QUICK TAKES: MOVIES AND POPULAR CULTURE

Quick Takes: Movies and Popular Culture is a series offering suc-cinct overviews and high quality writing on cutting edge themes and issues in film studies. Authors offer both fresh perspectives on new areas of inquiry and original takes on established topics.

Sports Movies

LESTER D. FRIEDMAN

RUTGERS UNIVERSITY PRESS

New Brunswick, Camden, and Newark, New Jersey, and London

Library of Congress Cataloging-in-Publication Data
Names: Friedman, Lester D., author.
Title: Sports movies / Lester D. Friedman.
Description: New Brunswick, NJ : Rutgers University Press,
[2020] | Series: Quick takes : movies and popular culture |
Includes bibliographical references, filmography, and index.
Identifiers: LCCN 2019019297 | ISBN 9780813599878 (hardcover) |
ISBN 9780813599861 (paperback) | ISBN 9780813599908 (pdf) |
ISBN 9780813599885 (epub)
Subjects: LCSH: Sports films—History and criticism. |
Motion pictures—United States—History and criticism. |
Sports in motion pictures.
Classification: LCC PN1995.9.S67 F75 2020 |
DDC 791.43/655—dc23
LC record available at https://lccn.loc.gov/2019019297

A British Cataloging-in-Publication record for this book is
available from the British Library.

∞ The paper used in this publication meets the requirements of the
American National Standard for Information Sciences—
Permanence of Paper for Printed Library Materials,
ANSI Z39.48–1992.

www.rutgersuniversitypress.org

Manufactured in the United States of America

TO EBEN HECKTOR
WELCOME TO THE FAMILY

CONTENTS

CONTENTS

SPORTS MOVIES

INTRODUCTION

Some games are purely random, but most follow rules
that blend skill and chance to keep things interesting.
Competition may call for strategy or strength, chal-
lenging competitors physically or mentally, thus building minds and bodies. Players may compete against a
personal best or head-to-head against opponents. But
competitive team play requires pulling together to win,
fortifying social bonds, and maximizing complemen-
tary skills.

—The Strong National Museum of Play
(Rochester, New York)

THE LOVE AND THE LOOT OF THE GAME:
AMERICA'S SPORTING CULTURE

From the point of view of a dispassionate onlooker, or
perhaps an alien on a first visit to Earth, all sports are
inherently stupid. Why should anyone waste time car-
ing about who can run faster, jump higher, or lift more
weight when any number of dire situations threaten our
world daily? This confused observer might assume that
only a madman thought it would be fun to jump headfirst

onto a tiny sled and plunge down an icy mountain as fast as possible—and without brakes. Our puzzled visitor would find it even harder to understand why crowds of people derive pleasure by watching two men punch and kick each other until one can no longer stand upright. Such potentially lethal activities would seem barbaric, and the onlookers cheering ringside would seem sadistic. Roughly calculating the extensive amount of prime real estate devoted to sports—the golf courses, tennis parks, athletic stadiums, football fields, soccer pitches, hockey rinks—this baffled visitor might wonder why these huge tracts of valuable land are not utilized for more socially beneficial functions, perhaps to raise food for hungry people or to provide housing for those who lack shelter.

Upon further exploration, our spectator would be stunned to discover the avalanche of revenue generated by sport activities. For example, WinterGreen Research reported (September 1, 2018) that six in ten children ages six to twelve regularly participate in team sports, helping to spawn a lucrative youth-sports industry currently generating revenues of over $17 billion per year in the US market ($22 billion worldwide). In 2018, the global sports industry was worth $620 billion and growing much faster than national gross domestic product (GDP) rates around the world (Collignon, Sultan, and Santander 1). Americans illegally wager an estimated $150 billion each year on professional and amateur sports, while another \$4.5 billion is bet legally (Kang). The salaries of the world's top-five athlete earners (Cristiano Ronaldo, \$93 million; LeBron James, \$86.2 million; Lionel Messi, \$80 million; Roger Federer, \$64 million; Kevin Durant, \$60.6 million) were augmented by endorsements totaling another \$209 million, and combined performance bonuses added yet another \$175 million to the total (Lauletta). Confronted by such almost-unfathomable numbers, our observer might ponder why people who can shoot a ball through a hoop, kick it into a goal, or hit it with a racquet command such huge sums and reasonably conclude that at no time in history have so many people paid so much money, spent so much time, and devoted so much emotional energy to engaging with contests that barely affect, and rarely change, their daily lives. Yet, however foolish, however illogical, and however dangerous, millions of individuals spend inordinate amounts of time, unseemly amounts of money, and excessive emotional energy rooting for a team, playing a sport, or buying sports merchandise.

But why? One answer to that question is that loyalty to a team begets great dollops of enjoyment. Watching a team that you and others support accomplish something exceptional generates a sense of collective pride. As part of a community of supporters, we find pleasure in witnessing a feat we thought to be improbable, or perhaps even impossible, just moments before it happened. By merely watching events unfold, we share the team's (or an individual member's) moment of triumph in accomplishing a feat that seemed so far out of reach for so long: fan and team, spectator and athlete, are linked together in a sliver of history the moment it happens—and long afterward as well. Collectively, we revel in the sensuality, the aesthetic beauty, and the natural grace of a body in motion, the instinctive delight in beholding an exquisite physicality that defies the limitations of gravity and the laws of physics as it coalesces into a visual harmony of person, time, space, and teammates. Such sparks of wonder and delight sufficiently dull more painful sports memories and allow us to continue rooting for a team or a particular athlete, despite the inevitable psychic wounds yet to come.

Devoted fans eagerly pursue information about their team, even in the offseason, and utilize multiple social media platforms—predominantly Facebook, Twitter, and Snapchat—to interact with others who share their passion; they avidly follow the dramas and melodramas that occur off the playing field as well as on it, cementing their bond virtually with each other in accessible meeting sites unconstrained by geographic borders. Rarely do members of these coteries refer to their chosen squads as separate entities, instead using personal pronouns like "we" and "us" that stress their oneness, their entrenched investment, with the objects of their loyalty. Thus, being a fan connects "personal identity to collective identity," and "media can become one part of a complex relationship that helps link an individual to a larger collective grouping" (Boyle and Haynes 13–14).

But what factors account for the chokehold sports retain on the public imagination? People seek escape from the pervasive corruption and injustice of the world in sporting events where the best, most prepared, hardest working athlete can prevail. As Doug Glanville notes, sports "on and off the field should set an example for fairness, decency and humanity for all of our children." Of course, they should; but they so often do not. Sometimes athletes or teams reap the just rewards for their discipline and dedication. Yet daily newspaper headlines and TV's "breaking news" cycles reveal a constant litany of everything from individual cheating to point shaving to financial payoffs to domestic violence to sex abuse scandals that provides scant reprieve from the pervasive corruption and injustice of the world. Equally evident, the journalistic boundaries that once segregated sports from our daily realities now cease to exist. Athletes are celebrities and, as such, face the scrutiny and wrath of the paparazzi horde eager to expose the clay feet of our current heroes.

In an era when the president of the United States slams NFL players for joining Colin Kaepernick to protest police brutality and racial inequality, it is wishful blindness to view sports as an apolitical escape from the events of daily life; the world of athletics has become—or maybe it was always—a dramatic microcosm of just how corruption, racism, violence, sexism, and injustice have infected our culture. As a result, the culture of sports is plagued by the same ills and problems that enflame the rest of American society, but its denizens find themselves pinioned under a far brighter spotlight. To be fair, we tend to hold athletes to a higher moral standard than allotted most other members of society, one particularly hard to maintain in a world flooded by an intrusive swarm of reporters anxious to feed a ravenous twenty-four-hour news and entertainment cycle that prior generations of athletes never had to navigate. But being a fan in the modern world means, at least for a brief time, having to ignore some of the most disturbing elements of the sports/media complex, tucking them securely into a gloomy corner of our mind—at least until we see who wins.

This book deals predominantly with US fictional team-sports feature films and offers something quite different from responding viscerally either to live sporting events or to sports movies. Exploring the thematic content and cultural significance of films whose narratives center on sporting events, whether based on historical facts or totally fictional, acknowledges the importance of the overflow of feelings but necessarily becomes a process that derives its strength, its worth, from the level and depth of analysis it brings to dissecting the subject. This book's investigation of sports movies, therefore, foregrounds analytical rather than passionate responses, critically exploring how these movies depict sports in a way that both refracts and reflects the central role that they continue to play in the United States' cultural and imaginative life.

"TELEVISION IS NOT THE TRUTH": SPORTS AND TV

Think of how many more sporting events you have watched on TV as compared to those you have attended in person. Most of us cannot scrape up money for Super Bowl tickets or find a way to attend the NCAA basketball finals, and so the vast majority of people in our sports-saturated environment consume athletic contests as mediated spectacles, mostly live and mostly on TV; in fact, the preponderance of our sports-viewing memories probably have been depicted and filtrated through media broadcasts that package and deliver games to our television screens. Because of this corporate and technological dominance, the network of interlaced connections that binds sports and television tightly together exerts a profound influence on the visual design, ideological content, and cultural context of sports film narratives, conventions, characters, and styles. What results, however, is a reversal of the traditional reciprocity pattern between TV and films. While television programs regularly mimic conventions initially established on movie screens, in this case most sports films necessarily take into account the techniques that TV directors routinely implement to present athletic competitions.

Watching most sporting contests on TV is a hybrid experience: an authentic event interlaced with staged elements and a scripted drama. On the one hand, the action on the field dictates much of the imagery that a viewer receives. But what parts of the ongoing action are shown and in what level of detail depend on what a director thinks viewers need to remain engaged. The games we watch on TV, therefore, substantially differ from attending athletic events in person, much as attending a live theater performance differs from viewing a filmed version of the same drama; in the former, you can observe whatever portion of the stage attracts your attention, but in the latter, a director dictates what and how you see what occurs on the screen. Similarly, the vantage point of an in-stadium spectator does not necessarily align itself with that of the viewer at home, although at times it certainly does so. While the announcer focuses mainly on play on the field, the broadcast's director determines what appears on your TV screen. For example, neither the familiar cuts to commentators bantering in the broadcast booth nor the swift pans of the cheering (often costumed) crowd are part of the in-stadium spectator's experience. Sports broadcasting integrates aspects of a carefully orchestrated event, since commentators have a general narrative outline: their research and preparation emphasizes certain key players and background situations, a set of opinions about various plays that will predictably appear, and some conventional back-and-forth chitchat. They inevitably highlight the basic narrative used to promote the event: for example, young Jared Goff versus veteran Tom Brady in the Super Bowl, LeBron James returns to Cleveland as a Laker, the defensive skills of Anthony Davis against the offensive proficiency of Kevin Durant.

In essence, then, TV fundamentally shapes how we conceptualize and configure sports: when we imagine and often remember sporting contests, we habitually employ the visual conventions, the types of standard structures and images, that characterize television productions. Thus, television's significant visual impact is crucial in thinking about sports movies. While many conventions of sports coverage derive from the longer history of narrative cinema, the standard that all serious—and some not so serious—sports movies strive to emulate is the semblance of authenticity exhibited in television broadcasts of live sporting events. These films must be "believable." If they do not feel sufficiently realistic to allow the willing suspension of our disbelief to click into action, then we usually cannot immerse ourselves in the movie. Viewers, either overtly or subconsciously, compare the action on the movie screen to what they have witnessed on TV watching actual games, and if the gap between them is too large, then the movie usually fails. The task for filmmakers, therefore, is to find actors who can credibly play sports or actual players who can act, and that often proves a difficult combination. Television has forced moviemakers to craft, at the very least, a veneer of believability for viewers to accept them as plausible depictions of a sport and its practitioners; this indispensable level of performance realism in films has increased as television's presentation of sporting events has become progressively more technically sophisticated and interactive.

SPORTS MOVIES AS A GENRE

In "The Work of Art in the Age of Mechanical Reproduction," the philosopher and cultural critic Walter Benjamin

observes that "the uniqueness of a work of art is insepa-
rable from its being imbedded in the fabric of tradition"
(223). But does the assemblage of fictional sports films
form a genre, part of the "fabric" of US cinema traditions
and a definable category like westerns or musicals? The
foundations of genre construction stretch back to Aris-
totle's formal differentiation among the various internal
properties of imitative modes (epic, lyric, and dramatic
poetry) in the *Poetics* (335 BC), and this classification
system allow producers, distributors, and consumers
to investigate and analyze almost all realms of creative
works. Although differences of scholarly opinions exist
about various genre issues, most commentators agree
that a continual fluctuation, in both form and content,
between repetitions and variations, formulas and innovations, commercially popular conventions and novel
deviations typifies the history of mainstream US cinema.
Genre works almost inevitably become amalgamated
productions replicating some recognizable structures and
conventions from the past, while simultaneously incorporating ingenuity and freshness drawn from the present.
But no reliable formula exists to calculate the appropriate balance between the typical and the original—and all
the variations in between them. Too many repetitive elements pile up trite clichés that bore the viewer; too many
departures from generic expectations confuse, frustrate,

or even irritate the spectator. In other words, filmmakers working within broad and distinguishable genre configurations reconceptualize familiar patterns and conventions by infusing them with their particular worldview and taking into account the concerns and technologies of the current historical period (see Friedman et al.).

INTERTEXTUALITY AND HYBRIDIZATION

Because audience members necessarily approach every film with a history of watching and interpreting previous ones, no movie exists in total isolation from the past. As with all cultural productions, therefore, films are by their very nature *intertextual*. This term means that every cinema production is shaped by our experiences and understandings of other films, both past and present. Contemporary movies continually invoke memories of preceding movies, making intertextuality a pervasive ingredient in all film making and viewing, particularly those within recognizable genres. These dialogues between the cinema that was and the cinema that is do not necessarily confine themselves within the same genre; they often disregard boundaries, migrate between formats, and transgress lines of critical demarcation. Filmmakers continually blend narrative and iconographic elements from various sources, crossbreeding movies into genre combinations that rarely reside exclusively in just one category, a process called *hybridization*. Such an understanding of genre's intertextuality and hybridization does not invalidate its significance in the sphere of creative artistry. It simply means genre categories should not straitjacket our understanding of the multiple possibilities within movies and that genres are not static entities. Quite to the contrary, they are fluid, open-ended, and responsive to social conditions. All the components that constitute genres are always in play, always available for revisiting, and always accessible for revising.

With these considerations about intertextuality and hybridization in mind, we can formulate a basic and logical definition of the sports movie for categorization purposes: a sports movie focuses on athletic contests, those who compete in them, and those whose lives revolve around them. Simple and clear, right? As noted earlier, almost all films contain multiple generic elements, so sports movies routinely incorporate conventions we recognize from other genres, particularly screwball and romantic comedies, crime and gangster movies, biopics and melodramas, social problem and romance movies, and sometimes even musicals. But to label a film as part of the sports movie genre, its action must center around athletic games. These competitions cannot be tangential to the plot and characters, such as Quidditch in the

Harry Potter movies; instead, they must function as the principal activity in the narrative, one that physically, psychologically, and emotionally consumes the main figures. To put it another way, the motivation for the protagonist's actions and his or her goal must be inextricably bound to the match (or matches) against opposing teams or individuals. The clear majority of sports films contain multiple game-playing scenes, but exceptions do occur. *Draft Day* (Ivan Reitman, 2014), for example, strikes me as a sports movie, although no one dons gear or plays football. The game can also be imaginary, as in *Rollerball* (Norman Jewison, 1975 / John McTiernan, 2005), or even video competitions, as in *Ready Player One* (Steven Spielberg, 2018), but it must have objective rules, specified uniforms, an end goal, and recognized winners and losers. At times, however, even this apparent clarity turns murky: do *The Hunger Games* (2012, 2013, 2014, 2015) movies belong in a sports film genre?

GENERIC NARRATIVES, CHARACTERS, ICONOGRAPHY

Most critics agree about the importance of three vital elements in discussing genres: (1) a series of common narratives, (2) familiar characters, and (3) a recognizable iconography. Various types of uniforms and equipment are both general components of athletic competitions and unique items endemic to specific sports: although balls and uniforms are common elements across the sports movie spectrum, different types of balls and distinctive styles of uniforms characterize individual sports and become intrinsic to the iconography of the sports movie. The same is true of characters and plots. That said, certain narrative arcs emerge across a variety of sport films, no matter the singular sport depicted. These function as interconnected master narratives that help to define the genre, and while the following is not an exhaustive list, these story lines all contain a generous helping of male bonding and personal/team transformations:

Individual salvation/redemption/renewal. A character does something dreadfully wrong, and his involvement in sport, usually as a player or a coach, allows him to atone for his transgression, regain his dignity, earn the admiration of teammates, and win the love of a good woman (who initially rebuffed him).

Team unity. Bickering teammates must learn to put aside their selfishness, overcome their individual disputes, and learn how to work together to win, despite racial and social differences.

Generational mentorship. Aging pseudofathers pass down their hard-earned wisdom to their wayward pseudosons, gaining success that eluded them in their younger years. Often these stories include talented but unruly athletes who must learn discipline and respect from their older mentors.

Pathway out of poverty. Working-class characters use sports to escape lives of poverty and stagnation, finding romance and/or masculine brotherhood as they obtain higher social status and upward mobility.

Small-town heroes. An outmanned team (usually at the high school level) from a rural setting accomplishes unexpected feats, thereby bolstering civic pride and uniting diverse elements of their community.

Moral victories. Despite losing an arduous contest, a team or an individual performs heroically, winning the hard-earned respect of opponents and the admiration of fans.

Miracle wins. Facing seemingly overwhelming odds, an underdog team or individual—one not given almost any chance for a victory—triumphs.

Beleaguered everyman quest. An often white, working-class man, one who is not athletically gifted, achieves a lifelong athletic ambition that no one thought possible, the just reward for his obsessive determination, personal sacrifices, and gritty hard work.

Oftentimes more than one of these master narratives appear in the same movie, and other genres share some of these basic story lines as well. In many of these plotlines, the people in power consider the protagonists as losers who lack the skills necessary to attain their lofty goals. When they do manage to triumph, we share their victory, perhaps remembering that at some point in our lives we too have been judged—unfairly we believe—and found wanting; by identifying with these characters, we garner some measure of vicarious consolation and retribution from the events unfolding on the screen. As such, sports movies often fill the need for morality tales that seek to inspire the viewer with their action revolving around someone, much like the viewer, who has overcome formidable odds, habitually wrapping their feel-good narratives in the mantle of "inspired by a true story."

Although a gamut of characters inhabits these plotlines across this genre, each sport has a distinctive cast of standard figures whose presence and actions signify that we are in the world of a specific sport. Such an array of familiar figures remains common within all the various genres, and the changes in their depiction help to situate films within the history of their category. These facsimiles become stock characters who fill in the background, add color and depth, and sometimes function as foils to the protagonist. In the sports film genre, these cinema counterparts, generally based on the real-world competitors who populate the fields of play, don the outfits, employ the paraphernalia, and imitate the activities of their models as best they can. Such figures, then, are easy to recognize, given their costuming and behavior within the narrative. We identify them as enhancing the atmosphere of a sports film, an important component of the filmmaker's attempt to achieve a level of verisimilitude, meant to match TV broadcasts, that marks the production as authentic and thus believable.

The same holds true for the visual composition of these films. "Sports," as asserted by Murray Pomerance, "is essentially cinematic. . . . It is naturally susceptible to cinematic treatment because it is inherently and densely consequential and inherently visual" (311). But when talking about the visual presentation of sports, the spectator sees only what the camera (under the control of the director) wants him or her to see and often quite differently from what is possible with the naked eye. Some shots are determined by the parameters of the game. You cannot visually present the fighting within a tightly enclosed boxing ring in the same way you can as action on an expansive soccer pitch. The size differences between the fields of action are just too substantial. That is not to say that a series of similar shots cannot be used. A close-up in slow motion can capture a pitcher's graceful delivery as well as the fluid movements of a jump shooter or the timing of a lithe wide receiver. But while the mechanism is potentially the same, the result is markedly different depending on the part of the game being filmed. In addition, auditory elements strike different resonances and come to be an important component of the mise-en-scène. Hearing a fastball slam into a catcher's mitt is quite different from hearing a basketball swish through a net, but these types of sound effects contribute to the filmmaker's ability to convey the feel of the game for the viewer.

"WOMEN WEAKEN LEGS": FEMALE ROLES IN THE SPORTS MOVIE

If one were asked to quickly name a synonym for athletes, my guess is that "jocks" would almost immediately come to mind. Such a term, of course, refers exclusively to men and, rather specifically, to a male's private parts and his sexuality. "Jocks" also becomes a shorthand representation of the attitude toward women in sport films. Almost forty years separate the original *Rocky* from its offspring *Creed*. Yet, as demonstrated by the advice that Mickey (Burgess Meredith) gives to Rocky Balboa in 1976 about women/sex and athletic competition, which he later passes on to Adonis Johnson (Michael B. Jordon) in *Creed* (2015), not much has changed as far as the attitude toward women in the sports film genre: "women weaken legs." In other words, stay away from them because they rob you of your strength. Over the decades, relatively few mainstream sports movies feature female leads, although a few notable exceptions include *National Velvet* (Clarence Grown, 1944), *Pat and Mike* (George Cukor, 1952), *Personal Best* (Robert Towne, 1982), *A League of Their Own* (Penny Marshall, 1992), *Girlfight* (Karyn Kusama, 2000), *Bend It like Beckham* (Gurinder Chadha, 2002), *Million Dollar Baby* (Clint Eastwood, 2004), *Ice Princess* (Tim Fywell, 2005), *Stick It* (Jessica Bendinger, 2006), *Whip It* (2009), and *Battle of the Sexes* (2017). Mostly, however, sport films brandish an ethos of manly virility by showcasing clashes between violent men who prove their manhood and achieve victory by being stronger and tougher than their opponents. And women (and by extension sex) are a dangerous distraction.

But family problems that impede the protagonist's quest for recognition, respect, and victory often develop in these stories. As evinced in numerous films, the strained relationship between men and their fathers (or substitute father figures) occurs far more often than rifts between men and their mothers; such films usually end with a soothing scene of reconciliation between dad and his son enjoying or playing a game together. Despite such emotional moments, men who display feminine traits, either physically or emotionally, are usually belittled as frail and fragile—or, even worse, as homosexual.

They lack the requisite skill necessary to compete successfully, as summarized in the ultimate insult that Ham
Porter (Patrick Renna) hurls at the rival baseball team's
leader in *The Sandlot* (David Mickey Evans, 1993): "You
play ball like a girl!" In other words, you are too weak and
unskilled, and consequently too vulnerable, to command
respect in this testosterone-powered culture that den-
igrates "feminine" traits. Women may be on the screen
for long periods of time in the sports genre, but they are
essentially stock characters who conform to traditional
female movie stereotypes, occupying roles roughly
equivalent to those found in classic westerns: the sexually
alluring whore or the supportively ethereal Madonna.

Women assist and encourage the athlete during difficult times or turn into another obstacle he must overcome on the path to victory: a recognizably conservative
version of the mother/whore dichotomy that features so
heavily throughout the history of US cinema. One grouping of female characters (mothers, wives, girlfriends)
offer their men reassurance, encouragement, and comfort
that aid them during their arduous quest. Their treacher-
ous counterparts, the sexy femmes fatales, lure the athlete
away from his objective by dangling the erotic thrills of
sexuality before him. The helpful women are emotional
handmaidens, while the dangerous women are land
mines. Both types are distractions who occupy spaces

well outside the field of competition, the only place these men experience true exhilaration, even ecstasy. Thus, the movie athlete never defines himself in relation to women but rather in competition with other men. He fits neither into the world of home and hearth that one cluster of women defines nor into the seductive bedroom that the other grouping of women inhabits. Early in *A League of Their Own*, for example, a frustrated Jimmy Dugan (Tom Hanks) states the situation concisely when exclaims, "Girls are what you sleep with after the game, not ... not what you coach during the game." Notice that Dugan does not use a personal pronoun to describe his bedroom partners; he sees them not as "whos" but rather only as "whats"—entities not worthy of consideration as individuals and surely not as ballplayers—although he eventually does change his mind.

While athletic success determines male identity in this genre, female identity, if considered at all, is derived almost totally from connections and interactions with men. The sad irony is that while the role of women in the sports film has remained relatively static, the advent of women within the offscreen world of athletic competition has witnessed remarkable growth. One cannot overestimate the revolutionary role played by the Title IX section of the Educational Act of 1972 in transforming the very foundations of our sports culture. A thirty-six-word clause that required equal access for women in all aspects of education, including athletics, Title IX inspired radical changes and initiated a series of profound conundrums in an athletic world dominated by men, issues that range far beyond the confines of the field. As a direct result of the increased participation of women in all levels of competition stimulated and supported by Title IX, female athletes in a variety of sports have emerged as cultural icons with mass-market appeal and have redefined conventional views of what constitutes an array of qualities traditionally associated with women: this new world of athletic participation for women since the advent of Title IX "broadens the range of gender roles to make activity and achievement beyond looks an ideal for women" (Heywood and Dworkin 163).

As growing scholarly attention has been paid to the male body as a territory of personal and social identity, so Michael Messner, among others, argues that "the female athlete—and her body—has become a contested ideological terrain" and that "women's movement into sport represents a genuine quest by women for equality, control of their own bodies, and self-definition, and as such, it represents a challenge to the ideological basis of male domination" (*Out* 32). Indeed, the testosterone controversy surrounding the South African intersex sprinter Caster Semenya, winner of two Olympic gold medals, will probably be just the first high-profile case to emerge as athletic federations (and courts) struggle with how to define who is and who is not qualified to compete as a woman. That said, one need only to look around most any campus, and certainly in any gym, to understand the radical change from the post–World War II era to the present time in what is now considered a healthy female body. There is, then, a striking mismatch between the conventional roles women often still play in the sports movie and the expanding participation of women in sports off the screen.

WE NEED TO TALK ABOUT KEVIN

Throughout the history of US cinema, especially during its studio era, particular actors became emblematic of specific genres, although all these performers appeared in a variety of different films. So, for example, fans associated John Wayne and Clint Eastwood with westerns, George Raft and Edward G. Robinson with gangster films, Gene Kelley and Fred Astaire with musicals, Cary Grant with sophisticated comedies, Boris Karloff and Bela Lugosi with horror films—just to name a few. Although many A-list performers starred in sports movies, one actor emerges as preeminent in the sports genre: Kevin Costner. Let me list his various sports films: *Chasing Dreams*

(Therese Conte and Sean Roche, 1982), baseball; *American Flyers* (John Badham, 1986), cycling; *Bull Durham* (Ron Shelton, 1988), baseball; *Field of Dreams* (Phil Alden Robinson, 1989), baseball; *Tin Cup* (Ron Shelton, 1996), golf; *Play It to the Bone* (Ron Shelton, 1999), boxing; *For the Love of the Game* (Sam Raimi, 1999), baseball; *The Upside of Anger* (Mike Binder, 2005), baseball; *Draft Day* (Ivan Reitman, 2014), football; *McFarland, USA* (Niki Caro, 2015), cross-country running. In addition to these onscreen performances, some in minor roles but most in starring parts, Costner has leant his voice to sports documentaries about horse racing (*Laffit: All about Winning* [Jim Wilson, 2006]), race-car driving (*NASCAR: The Ride of Their Lives* [Rory Karpf, 2009], *Petty Blue* [Mike Viney, 2010]), baseball (*Fastball* [Jonathan Hock, 2016]), and mixed martial arts (*The Hurt Business* [Rob Cohen, 2016]). In *When It Was a Game* (Steven Stern, 2000), he reads a poem about baseball, and he is interviewed in *Hollywood Pinstripes: The Yankees in the Movies and on TV* (Marino Amoruso, 2003). No other performer comes close to matching this catalogue of sports movies.

Looking over Costner's work, one can see a variety of attitudes toward sport but always a basic reverence for the game and an understanding that sports can be a life-changing, possibly transcendent, experience. Even the veteran catcher Crash Davis, the beloved cynic from

Bull Durham, demonstrates an entrenched devotion to the game by sticking around past his prime until he attains the minor-league home-run record—a feat that goes almost totally unrecognized—and navigating his way through the seedy underworld of baseball purgatory reserved for those who cannot make it to "the show." Two of the most famous speeches in any sports film appear in Costner movies: the first, the raucous "I believe" speech that Crash delivers to seduce Annie Savoy (Susan Sarandon) in *Bull Durham* and, the second, the so-called "Sermon on the Bleachers" paean about baseball reminding us of "all that once was good and could be again," delivered by Terence Mann (James Earl Jones) in *Field of Dreams. Tin Cup* provides one of the most illustrative examples of the "moral victory" narrative when, instead of laying up on the eighteenth hole—and achieving a near-miraculous win in the US Open—Roy McAvoy takes twelve strokes, followed by a dramatic hole in one, to lose the tournament but become immortal. At this writing, Costner has announced plans for yet another baseball movie. "I've got one more in me," he told Larry King during a 2016 interview, "and it has to do with the Cubs" (Landers). Play ball, Kevin!

If Kevin Costner reigns as the John Wayne of sports movies, then Ron Shelton emerges as the genre's John Ford. Shelton, a former minor-league baseball player, has written and/or directed films about various sports, including baseball (*Bull Durham*, *Cobb* [1994]), golf (*Tin Cup* [1996]), basketball (*White Men Can't Jump* [1992], *Blue Chips* [1994]), boxing (*Play It to the Bone* [1999], *The Great White Hype* [1996]), and football (*The Best of Times* [1986]), as well as an episode of the ESPN documentary series *30 for 30* about Michael Jordan's attempt to play professional baseball (2009). These productions all display a love of sports, but they also delve behind the headlines to explore the daily lives of athletes toiling at their trade outside the glare of the media. Ironically, these characters' love of and failures in athletic competition both ennoble and damage most of them to one degree or another. Yet athletics provides the only possible conduit to redress their disappointments and repair themselves, sometimes by replaying a crucial game, as in *The Best of Times*, and other times in direct competition, as in *Tin Cup*, *Bull Durham*, *Play It to the Bone*, and *White Men Can't Jump*. Although Shelton's writing and directing reveal a deep connection to sporting culture, he rarely shies away from the tawdry sins that stain the fabric of US athletics—the corruption, the racism, the gambling, the hype, the obsession, and the rule breaking. But his films, at their center, revolve around the efforts of characters to discover a way that sports can mend their frayed dreams with stitches of temporary victories.

"A LEVEL PLAYING FIELD":
SPORTS MOVIES AND THE AMERICAN DREAM

I hope I epitomize the American dream. For I came against long odds, from the ghetto to the very top of my profession. I was not immediately good at basketball. It did not come easy. It came as the result of a lot of hard work and self-sacrifice. The rewards, were they worth it? One thousand times over.

—Bill Russell

Although passionately invoked in prose and poetry, on the screen, and by a litany of political rhetoric, the "American Dream," built on a belief in our country's "exceptionalism," remains a slippery and multilayered ideological construct; nonetheless, this ideal plays a foundational rôle in forging the American ethos despite signifying different things to different people. Here is a bedrock belief that underlies most formulations of the American Dream: the United States was conceived of and actualizes a meritocracy, a level playing field overflowing with boundless opportunities to succeed. If you work hard, follow the rules, exert discipline, and undertake self-sacrifice, you can attain your highest aspirations: you can make the dream flesh. The novelist Richard Russo succinctly sums up the American Dream when he writes, "Probably no people embrace change more enthusiastically, at least in theory, than Americans. Who we are at birth is less important to us than who we will become. We are expected, indeed obligated, not just to be but to become" (139).

This optimistic creed, Emersonian in its ideals of confidence, hope, and self-reliance, also spawns a far-less-sanguine corollary, one that inspires fewer admired quotations but remains equally important to acknowledge. Because a dynamic American idealism posits that, as a free and democratic society, all our citizens are treated fairly and have an equal chance to pull themselves up by their bootstraps, the failure to succeed in our culture results not from any inherent defects in the system but instead from essential flaws, some missing psychological or emotional traits, in an individual's character. Entrenched racism or unyielding patriarchy or wealth disparities—all understood as particularized rather than systemic barriers—can be surmounted with sustained efforts and exertions of will. Failure to do so, then, is ascribed to the shortcomings, the weaknesses, of the person, not to the imperfections in the United States' social, economic, or political systems. "Look around," we're told; "others who faced even greater challenges have reached, and sometimes even exceeded, their ambitions. Why have they made it and you have not? What do you lack?"

From the foregoing description, you can see some obvious connections between the attainment of a sports victory and the fulfillment of the American Dream, both culminating in overcoming daunting impediments to win and thereby achieve recognizable success. Theoretically, at least, both are conceived of as a contest played on a neutral field of action; players/citizens possess self-determination and therefore the ability to carve out their own destinies; dedication, fortitude, self-sacrifice, and discipline are all indispensable to winning; clear rules are available, and those who violate them are punished appropriately; victory or defeat is dependent on and results from the behaviors of the individual; obstacles and barriers can be overcome; deserving athletes/citizens eventually triumph. Some detractors disparage these embedded precepts as fairy-tale homilies invoked by the masters of the capitalist universe to placate, and perhaps even control, the roiling masses. They characterize modern athletics as pseudo-"Hunger Games" that distract spectators from how the dominant class manipulates and abuses them. For these critics, "the major function of mass-produced sports is to channel the alienated emotional needs of consumers in instrumental ways" (Messner, *Out* 36); in other words, sports replace religion as the opiate of the masses.

That said, however, athletes who embody the archetypal "rags to riches" story, epitomized by Bill Russell's quote at the start of this section, authenticate the ideals of US society as a meritocracy; thus, they reap the considerable rewards due cultural heroes and assume the mantle of role models. So it would not be hyperbolic to claim that the American Dream and the Athletic Dream both incorporate the same set of fundamental attitudes, aspirations, and principles, a merging of sports and culture that could aptly be called the ESPNing of America. All that was needed to sear this vision of athletes as embodying the American Dream into the country's mythic imagination of itself was an influential and widespread delivery system. As Andrew Miller concludes, "Cinematic sporting culture, overall, continually reproduces the myth of the American Dream, and consistently represents and presents images of idealized American masculinity. . . . The Athletic American Dream seeps into the American consciousness during the nineteenth century, but it is not until it combines with the mass media technology of film that it gains widespread popularity . . . and helps to forge the masculine ideal that is the foundation of American self-image" (117–18). This "utopian sensibility" of the sports film, as Sean Crosson labels it (157), thus becomes deeply entrenched in US cultural life, stretching from the silent-film days to the latest multiplex feature. No greater exponent or purveyor of the American Dream exists than the sports movie. The vast majority of these American Dream / Athletic Dream films, even when they offer token criticism of its assumptions, still depict admirable icons who epitomize the American Dream: rugged individuals (or teams) working within a meritocracy composed of abundant opportunities where success or failure results from individual (or team) actions. Thus, "the fault," dear readers, "is not in the stars but in ourselves."

By offering a well-worn pathway to becoming a "socially acceptable minority," the hypnotic spell woven by merging the American Dream with the Athletic Dream is "particularly attractive to the marginalized and underprivileged," and "its representation had significant appeal for large numbers of recent immigrants to the United States, as well as members of the African American community" (Crosson 67). Indeed, the history of sports in the United States clearly exhibits the disproportionate presence of ethnic minorities and participants from impoverished backgrounds. The persistent representation of athletic competition in Hollywood movies, as Aaron Baker notes, emphasizes "the value of sports as a catalyst for upward mobility" (3). Throughout the history of this genre, movies depict sporting competitions and their participants as prototypical symbols of American success who rise from society's fringes to its center. "Sport thus is presented as a powerful validation of American social mobility, proving that in America you can choose to be what you want to be" (Babington 27).

These sports movies preach tolerance and acceptance as a two-way street. They depict an accessible conduit for newcomers to gain admittance into the higher echelons of US society and induce Americans to admire these newcomers first on the athletic field, then in schools, and finally as fellow citizens.

"PAIN DON'T HURT": MASCULINITY IN THE SPORTS FILM

As early as Buster Keaton's *College* (James W. Horne, 1927), sports movies dealt with issues of masculinity, as well as the inherent conflicts between athletic and academic cultural norms. Ronald (Keaton), a brilliant high school student, delivers an impassioned honors graduation speech titled "The Curse of Athletics," proclaiming that books, not sports, are important, that sports are a waste of time, and that future generations will depend on brains not brawn—a diatribe that causes his angry audience to storm out of the auditorium, leaving only his mother and the school's faculty to applaud. Later, the woman he loves (Anne Cornwall) and follows to Clayton College (an "athlete-infested" institution) tells Ronald that "anyone would prefer an athlete to a weak-kneed teacher's pet," an emasculating taunt that compels him to attempt various positions on the baseball squad and a slew of events on the track team, all abject (although humorous) failures; finally, inspired by an image of his beloved, Ronald leads the crew team to a stunning defeat of their hated opponents. In a brilliant traveling sequence, Keaton saves his future wife from a threatening athlete/rival (Harold Goodwin) by expertly performing all the athletic feats he previously failed to execute in his disastrous tryouts. Thus, the nerd performs like a jock to gain the respect and love of a woman, but the jock (who takes seven years to graduate high school) cannot duplicate the intelligence of the nerd and flunks out of college. Although *College*'s best athlete becomes the least likable character, the high school scholar almost fails out of college because he spends all his time trying to impress the woman he loves by joining a team, a testament to the lure of hyper-masculinity-that-leads-to-feminine-attention theme, a persistent concept deeply embedded in sports movies.

Most genre films that feature men in situations that require intense physical action, as do sports movies, offer highly stylized perspectives and assessments on what it means to be a man in US culture. In response to fluctuating social conditions, the qualities that constitute acceptable expressions of manhood get reshuffled over time, but such modifications and revisions occur less frequently in this genre than in most others. Basically, sports movies foreground an "aggressive masculinity" (Boyle and Haynes 193) that values toughness, strength, and discipline as the important traits a man must develop and implement to succeed as an athlete—and, it is implied, in life as well. Even competitors in sports like golf and figure skating, where the champions are not sculpted figures bulging with muscles, emphasize these qualities, as highlighted in commentaries and interviews with stars such as Tiger Woods and Adam Rippon. These portraits depict men behaving in a manner that some people would call nostalgic (men doing what men needed to do), that others label as retrograde ("And you knew what you were then, girls were girls and men were men"), or even as toxic misogyny ("site of white masculinism and racial, sex, gender, and class oppression"; Babington 9).

But, overall, representations of manhood displayed in sports movies have not changed substantially since the early days of the cinema as represented in Keaton's *College*, although the conditions and culture surrounding them clearly have done so. Seen in this way, sports heroes fall within a long tradition of men asserting their dominance on the battlefield of honor, whether they be knights, gunslingers, soldiers, or athletes; these rugged warriors fulfill one of society's most ancient and intrinsic needs—the hunger for a hero: "There's something primal about sports competition, urges and reactions tied up with threat, weakness, potency, domination" (Marzorati 21). As Baker and others have observed, sport films reassert an "ideal masculinity" as "a means of reaffirming and empowered masculinity" (52–53), and as Messner contends, they bolster "a challenged and faltering ideology of male superiority" (*Out* 32). Similar to fearless gunmen meeting at high noon or gallant soldiers storming enemy fortifications, athletes in sports films employ violence when demanded by their competitions, conform to prescribed codes of conduct, and preserve rather than undermine American values. They valiantly struggle to realize the American Dream, not destroy it, to be lionized by society, not blow it up.

But that acceptance is not always easy to accomplish because our culture delivers mixed messages about how men ought to behave, both on and off the field. Susan Bordo's nuanced analysis explores this "double bind of masculinity: gentleman or beast" (229); sports, she argues, celebrate male aggression and reconnect us with destructive primitive urges usually subject to cultural suppression. Even the language used to describe noncontact sports—one thinks of tennis, golf, and figure skating—emphasizes aggressiveness, power, and dominance. The highly rewarded behavior of the "warrior male" on the field, Bordo continues, "remains hard to control off the field" (236), particularly when modeled by athletes who occupy a lofty rung in our celebrity hierarchy. In this sense, then, sport activities in the modern world replace the ancient rituals of hunting and gathering as social rites of passage, practice, and identity for men. On movie screens, athletes define and embody masculinity, and the genre "valorizes, romanticizes, and rewards men's successful use of violence" (Messner, *Out* 91). These movies justify the public spectacle of violence by venerating those who use it skillfully in athletic competitions, an attitude that detractors decry as unhealthy for society. The rebuttal to such criticism, perhaps surprisingly, draws on the same defense offered by the proponents of pornography: these potentially dangerous impulses are expunged for the viewer/spectator by their enactment under the rubric of play, a culturally acceptable safety valve that triggers a necessary and healthy discharge of these desires in a harmless manner. In other words, viewing sports and sports movies allows us to acknowledge these potentially violent urges and to purge them from our systems by the vicarious identification with sports heroes, those mediated emblems of constructed masculinity who indulge in aggressive actions under safe, specified, and socially sanctioned codes of conduct that link both spectators and athletes back to patriarchal cultural norms.

Given this discussion of masculinity in US culture, it seems appropriate to briefly examine the connections between the sports movie and the genre that it most resembles: the combat film. Whether it·be Lord Wellington's famous claim that the Battle of Waterloo was won "on the playing fields of Eton," Stephen Crane using football games as the basis for combat scenes in *The Red Badge of Courage*, George Orwell characterizing the Olympics as "serious sport is war minus the shooting," or a raft of scholars exploring how war-inspired terminology and military metaphors describe sporting activities, lethal combat and sports remain enmeshed in the Western cultural imagination. Indeed, most historians believe that military training was the progenitor of sporting competitions arranged to develop an ancient soldier's physical strength and fighting skills; as a result, as discussed earlier, sporting competitions channel our violent instincts into nonlethal actions. Although much could be said about the connections that bind combat and sports movies together, in both genres men suffer severe pain and brutality—although in combat movies, they face death rather than simply defeat as in the sports movie. That said, the intense physical pain and suffering resulting from pushing the body beyond its utmost limits—often amplified in extensive training scenes for battle or competition—is another familiar trope that links sports and war movies with each other.

Because athletes have become foundational constitu-
ents of the American mythology, they function as aspira-
tional role models for those who are seeking to enact the
American Dream. They fulfill our collective craving for
heroes, invite us to share communal successes, conduct
us to the pastures of nostalgia, and help form our shared
identity. They also bridge differences. Extraordinary
physical feats on the fields of play become the stuff of
legends, ageless fables told and retold as one generation
hands them down to the next. On a personal level, most
of us have what Gerald Marzorati calls a "play history": "a
personal, emotionally complicated narrative of our childhood experiences of games and sports that we might find
useful to shape from our memories later in life" (45). But
athletes and their feats move beyond the personal. Film
and television productions anoint athletes as iconic illus-
trations of what our society deems, for better or worse,
some of the best parts of ourselves. As such, they seep
into the deepest strata of the US cultural imagination.
Although we remain aware of the assorted scandals, the
medical dangers, the retrograde politics, and the naked
greed that blight our sports culture, most of us still watch
and attend games, still marvel at the exquisite athletic
skills displayed on the field, and still revel in the reflected
glow of our team's triumphs.

1

BASEBALL MOVIES

> Baseball was a kind of secular church that reached into every class and region of the nation and bound us together in common concerns, loyalties, rituals, enthusiasms, and antagonisms. Baseball made me understand what patriotism was about at its best.... It seemed to me that through baseball I came to understand and experience patriotism in its tender and humane aspects.
>
> —Philip Roth, "My Baseball Years" (1973)

Although stadiums were built in cities, baseball has always projected the aura of a pastoral game played on grassy fields during sunny summer days, a sport that sprouted naturally from the soil that nurtured the United States' agrarian roots. And, as the writer Philip Roth observes, baseball (aka "America's National Sport") has played a considerable role in the American imaginary, particularly in the ways that Americans defined themselves and their country in the twentieth century. In particular, Roth emphasizes how baseball provides a common event that transcends the differences that divide Americans. In a famous routine comparing baseball and football metaphors, the comic George Carlin dissects the common language of each sport, comparing football's military metaphors to baseball's more comforting language, such as, "The object of the game is to be safe at home." Such musings situate baseball as a creaky anachronism in the modern world, a bucolic nineteenth-century game without time limits trying to adjust itself to a technologically driven twenty-first-century mind-set devoted to speed and impermanence.

Susan Jacoby's *Why Baseball Matters* (2018) contends that the qualities that this game demands—concentration, time, and memory—feel out of sync with our contemporary culture of "digital distractions" that routinely disrupt all three. Because baseball "derives much of its enduring appeal from a style of play and adherence to tradition," Jacoby continues (22), it fails to attract a sizable following of younger sports devotees who can choose among numerous high-tech entertainment options intently attuned to the hustle and flow of modern times. As a result, baseball's fan base is shrinking. With an audience mostly composed of white men over fifty-five, baseball games attract fewer female and African American watchers during its season than do NFL or NBA games and NASCAR races during theirs. Such a decline troubles some of baseball's most ardent supporters. In the 1954 book of essays *God's Country and Mine*, the cultural historian Jacques Barzun lavished praise on baseball, concluding, "Whoever wants to know the heart and mind of America had better learn baseball" (qtd. in Jacoby 15). But later in life, Barzun, disgusted with the sport's zealous embrace of commercialization and greed, recanted: "I've gotten so disgusted with baseball, I don't follow it anymore. I just see the headlines and turn my head in shame from what we have done with our most interesting, best, and healthiest pastime" (qtd. in McDaniel 1). Such head-shaking sadness, even antipathy, toward the current state of baseball is not an uncommon stance among those who once revered the game as representing the soul of the United States.

During the silent-film years, viewers watched clips of baseball games captured in newsreels while sitting comfortably in the movie theater, such as the Essanay Company's one-reeler of World Series highlights between the Chicago Cubs and the Detroit Tigers in 1908 and Selig Polyscope's four reels of the World Series between the Giants and the Athletics in 1913. Such productions allowed those who lived outside the environs of the ballparks to see baseball stars they read about in the newspapers, such as Babe Ruth, in action. Not surprisingly, therefore, making baseball movies appealed to early fiction filmmakers as well. In the late 1890s, Thomas Edison produced plotless one-reelers, such as *The Ball Game* (1898) and *Casey at the Bat* (1899), that capitalized on and further fueled the popularity of the sport. As films got longer, Biograph released *Play Ball on the Beach* (1906); Edwin S. Porter directed *How the Office Boy Saw the Ball Game* (1906); G. M. "Bronco Billy" Anderson's short film *The Baseball Fan* was often included as a part of vaudeville programs in 1908; and *His Last Game* (1909), about a Native American pitcher, appeared the same year. In films like *Spit-Ball Sadie* (1915), starring Harold Lloyd, comedy and baseball exist comfortably together. Rob Edelman, whose books include *Great Baseball Films* (1994) and *Baseball on the Web* (1998), describes the baseball films made during this era as a mirror to "the now long-extinct American culture before 1920: a time of innocence, a pre–Jazz Age America of small towns and small-town types. The prevailing view was that the simplicity of rural life was preferable to the corrupting ways of the metropolis. It was an era when filmmakers could celebrate a pastoral America whose foundation was Victorian morality, while emphasizing the notion that leaving the farm for the city meant going off in search of sin. . . . If baseball truly was America's national pastime, such baseball players were ideal all-American heroes" (qtd. in Thorn). A good example of these early movies is *The Busher* (Jerome Stern, 1919), the story of a talented small-town pitcher who finds life in the city as a professional ballplayer filled with far more obstacles and temptations (including women, gambling, and drinking) than had his innocent country life, and a rural/urban dichotomy becomes a convention in many subsequent baseball films. Treated as a rube by his new teammates, Ben Harding (Charles Ray) fails miserably in his debut before family and friends, leading him to flee in shame. Eventually, life offers him another chance to become a hero, as his hometown team faces its arch rivals and he redeems himself with his pitching and his hitting, regaining the respect of his father and love of his former girlfriend (Colleen More).

As the decades rolled on, Hollywood produced a relatively sparse but growing number of baseball movies: twelve during the 1930s, thirteen during the 1940s, and twenty from 1950 to 1958. Then, fifteen years slipped by with only one baseball movie. Considering the conspicuous gap between 1958 and 1973, when, other than the comedy *Safe at Home* (Walter Doniger, 1962), baseball movies essentially disappeared from movie screens (see Zucker and Babich), Vivian Sobchack speculates that it occurred "because the utopian national space previously figured by baseball on the screen was so completely at odds with the cultural upheavals in the America of the 1960s . . . and not yet ready to be nostalgically redeemed" (10). Before and following this hiatus, the vast majority of baseball movies in the sound era depict the game deferentially, paying respectful homage to its traditions and showcasing its players as larger-than-life, quasi-mythological figures. Biographies—such as *The Pride of the Yankees* (1942), *The Babe Ruth Story* (1948), *The Stratton Story* (1949), *The Jackie Robinson Story* (1950), *The Pride of St. Louis* (1952), *One in a Million: The Ron LeFlore Story* (1978), and *Fear Strikes Out* (1957)—all show their protagonists struggling with personal and professional problems but ultimately surmounting these obstacles to achieve their objectives; these "inspirational" narratives far outnumber more disparaging biographies presenting negative aspects of the sport, including racism and fixing games, for example, *Eight Men Out* (1988) and *Cobb* (1994), that render a far-less-flattering picture of their tainted players. Many of the fictional plotlines over the decades—seen in movies such as *The Adventures of Frank Merriwell* (1936), *The Kid from Cleveland* (1949), *The Kid from Left Field* (1953), *The Natural* (1984), *A League of Their Own* (1992), *The Sandlot* (1993), and *The Rookie* (2002)—follow a basically similar formula as do the majority of nonsports biopics: hard work and talent properly applied turn adversity into victory. Even films that take a more jaundiced look at the game show how players, coaches, or scouts who initially seemed jaded—as in *The Bad News Bears* (1976), *Bull Durham* (1988), *Major League* (1989), *Mr. Baseball* (1992), and *Million Dollar Arm* (Craig Gillespie, 2014)— eventually succumb to the purity, the inherent integrity, of the athletic contest and offer up their best efforts.

"YOU CAN'T TRY TOO HARD": *PRIDE OF THE YANKEES*

Pride of the Yankees (Sam Wood, 1942), cited by some commentators as the first great sports movie, tells the story of baseball's preeminent martyr: Lou Gehrig, nick-named "the Iron Horse." A seven-time all- star, Gehrig was a fearsome slugger—batting .340 over seventeen seasons, slamming 493 home runs, winning the Triple Crown, playing on seven World Series teams that won six titles—and he is usually considered the greatest first baseman in major-league history. But he remains most famous for playing in 2,130 consecutive games from 1925 to 1939, when at age thirty-six, he acquired the incurable neuromuscular disease amyotrophic lateral sclerosis— thereafter called "Lou Gehrig's disease"—and was forced to retire. His farewell speech, immortalized in this movie, concluded with the poignant line, "Today, I con-sider myself the luckiest man on the face of the earth," a quote as familiar to sports fans as lines from the Gettys-burg Address are to history majors. Released during the

United States' first full year in World War II, *Pride of the Yankees* provided audiences with an enduring archetype of an athletic hero who was struck down in the prime of life, a GI in pinstripes who confronted tragedy stoically. Gehrig became the incarnation of American manhood and a model for those American boys facing death on faraway battlefields. We never see Gehrig in the final, degenerative stages of his life, and the movie ends with his leaving his beloved Yankee Stadium for the last time, accompanied by the cheers of over sixty thousand fans. The plaintive melody of "Always" lingers throughout the film's soundtrack, reminding viewers, "Days may not be fair / But I will be there always," a summation of Gehrig's idealized courtship and marriage to Eleanor (Teresa Wright), a loving relationship doomed by a terrible ailment that they face bravely together.

As such, *Pride of the Yankees* remains a paradigmatic example of the Hollywood baseball film of this era. As one of Hollywood's biggest stars, Gary Cooper had already gained fame playing heroes in *Mr. Deeds Goes to Town* (Frank Capra, 1936) and *Sergeant York* (Howard Hawks, 1941), by the time he embodied Gehrig on the screen. (Although Cooper was a right-hander and Gehrig battled left-handed, the magic of Hollywood prevailed, as Cooper relates: "The letters on my uniform were reversed as it is in mirror-writing and the film was processed with the back side to the front. My right hand thus appeared to be my left"; qtd. in Sandomir 135).

The studio hired the sportswriter Damon Runyon to explicitly connect the film to the war effort, and his patriotic words scroll across the screen to start the movie: "This story is a . . . lesson in simplicity and modesty to the youth of America. He [Gehrig] faced death with the same valor and fortitude that has been displayed by thousands of young Americans on far-flung fields of battle. He left behind him a memory of courage and devotion that will ever be an inspiration to all men." The film explicitly espouses a staunch faith in the American Dream, when Mama Gehrig (Elsa Janssen), a German immigrant, tells her son, "In this country you can be anything you want," and encourages him to attend Columbia University to become an engineer—a plan Lou rejects when the Yankees offer him enough money to pay her medical bills. When Gehrig and Babe Ruth (who plays himself) visit a sick child in the hospital, the Bambino plays it up for publicity photos, but Gehrig makes a personal connection with the child, telling him, "There isn't anything you can't do if you try hard enough"—again words that characterize a vital element of the American Dream.

Throughout the movie, Gehrig is characterized by his sports writer friend Sam Blake (Walter Brennan) as a working-class hero: "A guy who does his job and nothing else. He lives for his job. He gets a lot of fun out of it. And fifty million other people get a lot of fun out of him, watching him do something better than anyone else ever did it before." When Lou and Elsa marry, it is not a fancy celebration; they are joined by family, friends, and the blue-collar workers building their house. When Lou is late coming home, Elsa finds him umpiring a baseball game for some local kids. Such sentimental moments cement Gehrig into the role of the Everyman who works hard, is granted great gifts, and then has them tragically taken away from him. A modest Gehrig responds to both his good fortune and his bad luck with a laconic acceptance of life's fluctuations. It is, however, significant to remember that during this time so nostalgically invoked by so many Americans, major-league baseball was a totally segregated sport. Off the screen, the lofty sentiments of the United States as a country of opportunity for those who are willing to work hard to achieve their dreams, expressed by Lou and his mother, would have struck many Black ballplayers merely as empty platitudes with little applicability to their lives.

"THE CHURCH OF BASEBALL": *BULL DURHAM*

Pride of the Yankees represents a period of baseball movies that stretches from the 1930s to the end of the 1950s, one that incorporates the typical Hollywood stereotypes and narrative conventions that dominated US cinema during the studio era. *Bull Durham*, however, typifies a more raucous and cynical period from the 1970s onward, when fans proved unwilling to ignore the disparities between the lofty myths and the daily realities that constitute a professional athlete's world, including movies such as *Bang the Drum Slowly* (John D. Hancock, 1973), *Eight Men Out* (John Sayles, 1988), *Major League* (David Ward, 1989), *The Babe* (Arthur Hiller, 1992), and *The Rookie* (John Less Hancock, 2002). While these movies still revere the sport, they replace pious sentiments and nostalgic romanticism with dying athletes, crooked ballplayers, corrupt owners, and drunken legends, generating a sharp conceptual shift in how the game and its players are depicted. For example, marketing and profits are omnipresent: "a bright array of commercial products and logos has entered the generally pastoral and timeless space of baseball [that] connects the game and players not only to the commodified social space around them, but also to the commercial logos that increasingly substitute for the symbolically impoverished, traditional icons of nationalism" (Sobchack 13). Crash Davis (Kevin Costner), for all his appeal, is no Lou Gehrig, either in his athletic talent or in his pristine character. About thirty minutes into *Bull Durham*, for example, the team's batboy implores Crash to "get a hit." His grumpy response is, "Shut up!" A sly and knowing parody of the famous sick kid in the hospital scene in *Pride of the Yankees*, this quick scene provides recognition that, in tune with the turbulent 1960s and '70s, this is a far-less-heroic era than evoked in previous baseball movies but one containing a greater ring of truth and authenticity.

This is not to say that baseball's more fabled claims are absent or that Crash and his teammates love the game any less than did their celluloid predecessors. *Bull Durham's* opening monologue, spoken by Annie Savoy (Susan Sarandon), grandly binds religion, sex, and baseball together, as she claims that "the only church that feeds the soul, day in and day out, is the church of baseball." But rather than concentrating on the glamorous side of the game, the major leagues ("the show"), with its creature comforts, coddled players, and beautiful women, *Bull Durham* foregrounds the hardscrabble lives of blue-collar ballplayers who inhabit the minor leagues, a grubby underworld of decaying locker rooms, long bus rides, bush-league stadiums, fast-food restaurants, and two-lane country roads. It is a period of "prolonged adolescence," as Tim Robbins says in the "Extra Innings" section of the DVD, a short stretch of frozen time when men can still act like boys but finally must hang up their spikes, abandon the game they love, and assume more mundane pursuits.

But for all the film's brashness, its liberated female figure, its X-rated language, and its heated sexuality, *Bull Durham* still espouses much the same fundamental ideology as does *Pride of the Yankees*, particularly the need for players to realize their part, be it large or small, in the hallowed tradition of baseball and that the game, boiled down to its essence, is three simple acts: "You throw the ball. You hit the ball. You catch the ball."

As in *Pride of the Yankees*, a love story also exists along with the baseball action in *Bull Durham*, but instead of the virginal devotion between Lou and Elsa, the film offers Annie's sexually charged affairs. She chooses a player to have sex with and to mentor each year: first Nuke LaRoosh (Robbins), a rookie with a "million-dollar arm and a five-cent brain," and ultimately Crash, a world-weary catcher with twelve years in the minors trying to break the league home-run record—a feat few know about and even fewer care about. The plotline reaches back to a standard story of a young man with tons of talent and little discipline needing to be mentored by an older man who teaches him to harness his gifts and respect the game. At first antagonists, these men come to share a bond of trust that grows between one who has a chance at greatness and the other who knows he will never return to "the show." Despite Annie's interpretation that such macho bonding is just "latent homosexuality rechanneled," the two men come to recognize the strengths of the other. Crash even teaches Nuke how to employ sports clichés effectively, which he aptly demonstrates when he arrives in the majors, and to always approach the game with "fear and arrogance." Despite Annie's smoldering, libidinal presence, however, attitudes toward women sometimes retreat to tired clichés, such as when Crash warns Nuke that a woman's "pussy is like the Bermuda triangle. A man can get lost in there and never be heard from again." He also decrees that as long as Nuke and the team are winning, his protégé cannot have sex, a plot to keep Nuke from Annie but a note to superstitious players as well. Women may not weaken legs in *Bull Durham* as in *Rocky*, but apparently they weaken arms and destroy winning streaks.

"GO THE DISTANCE": *FIELD OF DREAMS*

Bull Durham foregrounds the raunchy side of baseball, but the cornfield mysticism and idealized rendering of agrarian life in *Field of Dreams* turns baseball into a metaphoric and, within the film's narrative structure, a literal passageway that allows its characters a second chance. As such, all the film's characters take advantage of a magical opportunity afforded them (and we are never sure why them and by whom) to correct a wrong or redress a substantial error that has haunted them for a lifetime. Here, amid the bucolic landscape of golden crops and hypnotizing sunsets, everyone gets a "do over" to amend their mistakes: Ray Kinsella (Kevin Costner) reconciles with his father (Dwier Brown) and saves his farm/family; Terence Mann (James Earl Jones) regains his passion for writing; Doc "Moonlight" Graham (Frank Whaley / Burt Lancaster) gets his big-league at-bat, the Chicago White Sox take to the diamond free of scandal, and Shoeless Joe Jackson (Ray Liotta) gracefully roams the outfield once more. A brief history lesson to contextualize this moment: Shoeless Joe Jackson played in the major leagues from 1908 (initially with the Philadelphia Athletics) until 1920, when Kenesaw Mountain Landis, the commissioner of baseball, slapped him and seven of his Chicago White Sox teammates with a lifetime ban for fixing the 1919 World Series, even though a jury acquitted Jackson of wrongdoing in 1921. Myth has it that following Jackson's trial, a disappointed kid greeted him outside the courtroom and begged him, "Say it ain't so, Joe." Jackson has the third-highest career average in major-league history, .356, and batted an astounding .408 in 1911. He has gone down in baseball history as a great player unfairly subjected to an overly harsh penalty, a victim, not a cheater.

More than only about individual reconciliations, however, *Field of Dreams* finds a path for the children of the turbulent '60s to understand their parents, and the sacrifices they made, through a mutual love of baseball. Those kids whose knee-jerk reaction was to reject whatever their parents held most dear, as represented by Ray, come to view their elders with more compassion and understanding, particularly since they now occupy roles formerly held by their parents. That is the "dream" this movie evokes, not of seeing long-dead ballplayers on a field in the middle of Iowa but of sharing the love of baseball—or of anything else—that establishes an intimate connection between fathers and their sons who can express their feelings for each other through talking about and sharing sports. Few men would not relish the chance to play catch with their dads, to have known them, even for a moment, as Rays says, before they were "worn down by life." How many grown-up sons do not yearn to tell their fathers that now, with children of their own, they better understand the decisions of the older man, the sacrifices he felt compelled to make for the good of the family? One of the reasons *Field of Dreams* remains such a fan favorite is because it allows viewers to play out this primal fantasy of fathers and sons reconciling while sitting inside the theater or at home.

Before leaving idyllic Iowa, however, some attention must be given to one of the most repeated speeches in the history of the baseball movie: Terence Mann's dramatic

monologue, an oft-quoted paean to baseball's longevity.
Mann's speech drips with honeyed nostalgia. He tells
Ray that people will show up in his driveway "as innocent as children longing for the past." They will sit in the
bleachers in "their shirtsleeves on a perfect afternoon ...
where they sat when they were children and cheered their
heroes." They will, he continues, "watch the game as if
they dipped themselves in magic waters," and their memories "will be so thick they'll have to brush them away
from their faces." He then turns to baseball itself, calling
it "the one constant through all the years." The United
States has been built and rebuilt, he asserts, but "baseball
has marked the time. This field, this game: it's a part of
our past. . . . It reminds us of all that once was good and it
could be again." But good for whom?

The era that Mann so fondly recalls was surely not
good for African American ballplayers, those outstanding
athletes denied any chance to play in the major leagues by
the overt prejudice and widespread racism of the game's
owners, players, and fans. While Joe Jackson's playing
days witnessed no integration of the races, the period
during which *Field of Dreams* was released certainly did;
so why no Black ballplayers or at least mention of this
racial bigotry, this blight on Mann's idealism? Is there
another cornfield stuck behind the region that Jackson
and his teammates inhabit, one crammed with great ath-

letes from the Negro League? Is Satchel Paige hurling fastballs back there? Is Josh Gibson belting home runs into the Iowa sky? For all the romanticism of Mann's sentiments, it remains a startling irony to hear a Black man playing the role of an ardent fan recite these wistful lines as if unaware of this ugly chapter of baseball's history. This was also a time when baseball players were, essentially, indentured servants to team owners, long before Curt Flood's courageous fight for free agency in 1969. Mann's famous speech, then, provides an apt illustration of how sports films paper over history's warts with sentimentality: to label those bygone days as a time that "once was good" without at least a sliver of recognition that they "once were bad" as well is to excuse the actions of those with power, money, and influence who yearn to enshrine their world in amber, preserving it immune to the forces of change and ignoring the plight of those who are denied access to the field of dreams.

"LOSING IS A DISEASE": *THE NATURAL*

Field of Dreams was not the first film to infuse magical realism into baseball. With a history stretching back to the days of yore, some earlier films employ the same narrative formula: *It Happens Every Spring* (Lloyd Bacon, 1949), *Angels in the Outfield* (Clarence Brown, 1951),

Roogie's Bump (Harold Young, 1954), *Damn Yankees* (George Abbott and Stanley Donen, 1958), *Angels in the Outfield* (William Dear, 1994), and *Angels in the Infield* (Robert King, 2000). But whereas *Field of Dreams* and these others confine their magical realism to relatively small canvases, *The Natural* (Barry Levinson, 1984) expands it into the realm of the mythical; its blend of magical realism with traditional themes and its exquisite cinematography remain key ingredients that enable the film to retain a lofty spot on any roster of the best base- ball films. Even though it reverses the tragic conclusion of Bernard Malamud's 1952 novel on which its based, *The Natural*'s climactic scene remains one of the most iconic and best loved segments in the history of sports films. On the page, it sounds like a collection of stale clichés: it is the bottom of the ninth, two outs, two on, and the New York Knights are down 2–0 in a playoff game. A jagged flash of lightning slices across the darkening sky. The injured Roy Hobbs (Robert Redford), facing an 0–2 count with his handcrafted bat cracked in two, blasts a towering three-run homer that, quite literally, knocks out the stadium lights. He rounds the bags accompanied by Randy Newman's triumphant musical score and the full- throated cheers of the hometown crowd, including his boyhood sweetheart and their son, as a glittering cascade of shattered glass showers him and his teammates like a rainstorm of birthday candles. The ball he hit travels, magically, through time and space, landing in his son's glove, re-creating the opening scene of Roy and his father playing catch and placing "the natural" back in the sun-drenched fields of his youth, a rural setting beyond the tentacles of urban corruptions. It should not work, but somehow it does.

The Natural features three women, usually dressed symbolically either in white or in black. The first, Iris Gaines (Glenn Close), is the childhood love whom Roy abandons but who appears later in the film to offer him salvation. Watching him struggle during a batting slump, she rises majestically in the stands, the light reflecting off her white outfit, and provides him with the touch of magic necessary to continue his fantastical odyssey. He meets the second, Harried Bird (Barbara Hershey), on his way to try out for the majors and, seduced by her physical allure, forfeits sixteen years of his life when she shoots him. The last, Memo Paris (Kim Basinger), also ensnares him with sexual pleasures, but she becomes a puppet doing the bidding of Roy's enemies. Thus, as in many of the sports movies, *The Natural* depicts the negative influence of women on athletes, particularly their sexual power that robs men, quite literally, of their strength and derails them from their commitment to victory. It is the Samson and Delilah (or, if you wish, the Adam and Eve) myth repackaged for modern audiences: with the seductive power of ancient Sirens, these dangerous women bewitch men and lure them to their ruin. *The Natural*, however, provides an alternative to these enchantresses, a woman dressed as virginal as a bride who reminds the protagonist of his farm-bred past and deep connection with his father, endowing him with the psychological strength necessary to succeed despite the powerful forces aligned against him. As Roy tells us, "A father makes all the difference."

An avaricious Judge (Robert Prosky) who hates the "infernal" light; a gambler (Darren McGavin) with a grotesquely enlarged eye; a sneering sports writer (Robert Duvall) with a jaundiced worldview—together they form a triumvirate of greed, corruption, and cynicism designed to crush men who revere the integrity of sport: Roy; Pop Fisher (Wilford Brimley), the beleaguered manager of the Knights; and Pop's faithful assistant coach, Red Blow (Richard Farnsworth). Early in the film, Harriet tells Roy that baseball players resemble the fabled figures in Homer's epic poetry, those venerated heroes and gods who became enshrined in legends. Indeed, many critics read Malamud's novel in relation to ancient myths, such as the *Odyssey* and the tales of King Arthur, and Roy's feats stretch beyond the reach of mortal men. In one scene, for example, he launches a homer into the stadium clock, quite literally stopping time, while in another, he smacks the ball so hard that he tears off its hide. The film does little to dispel these mythological echoes. But it also contains familiar elements, such as the agrarian-versus-urban dichotomy, as well as fathers and sons seeking reconciliation, that also appear prominently in *Field of Dreams*. As Malamud himself put, it *The Natural* turns history into myth.

"THE HARD IS WHAT MAKES IT GREAT": *A LEAGUE OF THEIR OWN*

The films in this chapter have focused on mostly white male characters whose obstacles involve their own athletic talent and character flaws. Outsiders who must also face societal prejudice, including women and African Americans, rarely emerge as the focus of baseball movies, mostly filling in the background either as teammates or, as we have seen, as wives, girlfriends, and lovers. In *A League of Their Own*, however, women move from the stands to the field. The All-American Girls Professional Baseball League, founded by major-league owners to keep baseball alive during World War II when their stars were in the service, operated from 1943 to 1954. It provided six hundred women (no African Americans were allowed to try out) a chance to compete and attracted up to nine hundred thousand fans during its peak 1948 season. Pictures taken during that time show the women in uniforms mimicked in the film, tunic-like dresses ill suited to the physical rigors of the game. Director Penny Marshall employs many of the tropes found in baseball movies starring men but often with a sly twist. Resembling many other baseball productions, this one begins in a beautiful rural setting and features working-class protagonists, but Willamette, Oregon, is clearly a dead end for Dottie Hinson (Geena Davis) and her younger sister, Kit Keller (Lori Petty). Dottie, a talented catcher and fearsome slugger, waits for the return of her husband, Bob (Bill Pullman), while Kit, a volatile pitcher, becomes nearly invisible in the lengthy shadow of her more athletically gifted and beautiful sister. Together, they successfully try out for the women's professional league and play as teammates on the Rockford Peaches. Their manager, a formerly great but now perpetually drunk former big leaguer, Jimmy Dugan (Tom Hanks), initially refuses to help the team and issues various sexist taunts ("Stop thinking with your tits!"), but he eventually recognizes their talent, particularly Dottie's skills, and the love of the game the women display each time they take to the diamond.

Although *A League of Their Own* offers positive images of women passionate about sports, it also sends a series of mixed messages, both inside its narrative and beyond it. So, for example, the film's central figure and ostensibly the league's best player, Dottie, plays with dexterity and intensity but claims that baseball "was never that important" to her and almost quits (and does miss six crucial games) before the final game in the World Series to go back to Oregon with her husband. Their cleanup hitter, Marla Hooch (Megan Cavanagh), does leave in the middle of the season. When Jimmy tells Dottie that "baseball is what gets inside you," she merely responds, "We're different," and when Kit says she will miss all this—playing only one season in the league—Dottie responds that all she will regret is being with the other women, the camaraderie, not the game itself. By including these seeming contradictions, Marshall depicts the pressure that women athletes were under at that time, the ambivalent feelings that even the best players felt about competing in a domain overwhelmingly dominated by men who considered them trespassers. Those female intruders who loved sports created "sexual confusion" and were judged to have something wrong with them, as Doris (Rosie O'Donnell) states it; indeed, most of these women, other than the promiscuous "All the Way" Mae Mordabito (Madonna), have never attracted much male attention beyond derision. But the film foregrounds other issues unique to women athletes too, such as child-care problems, sexist attitudes and stereotypes (the players are required to attend charm school) that force them to conform to traditional images of femininity, and desperate fears about their soldier-husbands' well-being. Like the "Rosie the Riveters" who took over the factory jobs while the boys were fighting in Europe and the Pacific, these ballplayers will soon be compelled to resume more traditional feminine roles, most going back into their homes as wives and mothers, once the men return to claim their rightful position on the field.

"AIN'T GONNA SHINE FOR NO WHITE FOLKS": THE BINGO LONG TRAVELING ALL-STARS & MOTOR KINGS

Similar to the women in *A League of Their Own*, the Black baseball players in *The Bingo Long Traveling All-Stars & Motor Kings* (John Badham, 1976) face social barriers beyond their control that even their talent cannot defeat, in this case racism. Although excellent documentaries and books—such as *There Was Always Sun Shining Someplace: Life in the Negro Baseball Leagues* (Craig Davidson, 2003), Lawrence D. Hogan and Jules Tygiel's *Shades of Glory: The Negro Leagues and the Story of African-American Baseball* (2006), Robert Peterson's *Only the Ball Was White* (2008), The "5th Inning" segment of Ken Burns's PBS series *Baseball* (2010), and *Pride and Perseverance: The Story of the Negro Leagues* (Jon O'Sheal, 2014)—

record the history of Negro-league baseball, *Bingo Long* is the only feature-length film to focus on this less-than-heroic period of segregated baseball history. As a result, it contains far more actors of color in key roles than do most other Hollywood baseball movies, limiting white performers only to secondary and nonspeaking roles. The film's major characters include fictional representatives of the two most famous African American players of that era, Satchel Paige (Bingo Long / Billy Dee Williams) and Josh Gibson (Leon Carter / James Earl Jones), along with a far-from-accurate portrayal of Jackie Robinson (Esquire Joe Callaway / Stan Shaw). The flamboyant but talented team includes Richard Pryor as Charlie Snow, a right fielder so obsessed with playing in the majors that he undertakes to pass himself off as a Cuban and, when that fails, as a Native American. Being demeaned and cheated by greedy owners, Bingo and Leon follow the advice offered them by W. E. B. DuBois and "seize the means of production" in order to "be their own men." They quit their teams, collect a group of Negro all-stars, and barnstorm across the South, playing local teams and dividing up the profits equally.

"Who's . . . gonna hit . . . my . . . invite pitch?" yells out Bingo from the pitcher's mound, and the delighted crowd echoes back his words. Starting with this call-and-response, so prevalent in African American cultural tradition (McDaniels 130), *Bingo Long* reveals this racist period in US baseball with a light, some would argue far too shallow, touch, highlighting the camaraderie between the team members and their athletic talent; but the film clearly shows the ugly prejudice of the white crowds when they play (and inevitably beat) their hometown teams. To forestall the possibility of violence—and the risk of lynching is mentioned several times—the team becomes a baseball version of basketball's Harlem Globetrotters. Out of necessity to earn their paltry paychecks and to escape with their lives, they develop an array of gags, some of which recall racial stereotypes, such as pitching in a gorilla suit, and other gimmicks like a midget catcher and a one-armed first baseman. These showboating tactics could easily be characterized as "shucking and jiving," thereby situating the actions in the tradition of Stepin Fetchit, but the film militates against such a harsh reading; instead, the team strutting and cakewalking down the main streets of small towns in their glitzy uniforms demonstrates the inherent ties between sports and show business, much as did *A League of Their Own*, as well as the desperate lengths Bingo and his team will go to play their beloved sport. At the end of the film, Bingo tells Leon that they are "the pinnacle of baseball creation," but a sad irony hangs over this statement. Once Esquire goes to the big leagues, the Negro league will shortly implode, as the best players opt to play within an integrated major-league structure. The great athletes of the Negro leagues, those too old to make the transition to the majors, will become images captured in black-and-white newsreels and wrapped in the shrouds of history, victims of an vile time in US history mirrored in its national game.

BASEBALL PAST ITS TIME

Whatever baseball's evolving status in the current bouillabaisse of US sport, culture, commerce, and entertainment, its storied history and its integral role in the formation of the American identity remains unmatched by any other sport. And filmmakers still find themselves drawn to stories about those who struggle inside the diamond. During the 2000s, for example, some forty baseball movies were released, including biographies (*The Rookie, 42* [Brian Helgeland, 2013], *Spaceman* [Brett Rapkin, 2016]), comedies (*Mr. 3000* [Charles Stone III, 2004], *The Benchwarmers* [Dennis Dugan, 2006], *Everybody Wants Some!!* [Richard Linklater, 2016]); dramas (*61** [Billy Crystal, 2001], *Sugar* [Anna Boden and Ryan Fleck, 2008], *Moneyball* [Bennett Miller, 2011], *Million Dollar Arm*), and romantic comedies (*Summer Catch* [Michael Tollin, 2001], *Fever Pitch* [David Evans, 2005], *Trouble with the Curve* [Robert Lorenz, 2012]). (TV also continues to produce outstanding documentaries that explore various aspects of the sport.) Well-known performers take on prominent roles in these feature films, such as Keanu Reeves, Dennis Quaid, Matthew Modine, Michael Keaton, Jimmy Fallon, Nick Nolte, Clint Eastwood, Ed Harris, Jeff Bridges, Justin Timberlake, Owen Wilson, Reese Witherspoon, Harrison Ford, Jon Hamm, and Kurt Russell. It seems unlikely that baseball will regain its position as the most popular sport in the United States, but it remains a vital part of the national athletic scene and, with the heavy influx of Hispanic players, seems well positioned to take advantage of the shifting demographics in the ethnic composition of the country.

2

BASKETBALL MOVIES

[Obama] saw in basketball what he saw in jazz, an inef-
fable artistic expression of what it meant to be black and
cool, a brother.... With equally strong roots in the Kan-
sas of his ancestors and the playgrounds of black America, basketball connected the disconnected parts of him.
—David Maraniss, *Barack Obama: The Story*

In *The Audacity of Hoop: Basketball and the Age of Obama*
(2015), Alexander Wolff notes how Barack Obama, the
first president to play a team sport regularly while in
office, displayed his basketball skills as a campaign tool
to dispel fears that he was not truly an American, and as
president, he converted the White House tennis facility
into a basketball court. Here he played intense pickup
games, sometimes with NBA current all-stars like Car-
melo Anthony and LeBron James, as well as hosted legends like Bill Russell and Magic Johnson. In his boyhood,

as Obama said during his visit to Kogelo, Kenya, "One of the great things about sports . . . is what matters is not who you know, or who your father is, or how much money you have, but what matters is if you can play"—this from a man who barely knew his own father. Indeed, a basketball was the only gift that Obama's father gave his ten-year-old son during the one month they spent together, and as Obama notes in *Dreams from My Father* (1995), our forty-fourth president made his closest white friends on a court where the color of his skin could not be a disadvantage. This story, while extraordinary because of the heights Obama reached, is not unique; it is, rather, an archetypal story for many children, mostly African Americans but not exclusively so, who found in basketball the validation and acceptance that was in short supply within other parts of their lives.

Baseball evokes pastoral memories of grassy fields and dusty dirt base paths, of leisurely summer days with friends playing together in a game with no time limit, no set ending, until mom called out for dinner. In contrast, basketball is an urban sport contested on concrete courts outdoors and hardwood floors indoors. Games feature slashing moves that leave hapless defenders grasping at air, booming dunks over the outstretched arms of humiliated giants, and balls swatted away from their seemingly inevitable target—all accompanied by the soundtrack of sneakers squeaking, nets swishing, and balls bouncing. Time is carefully monitored during these games, and someone must take a shot every thirty seconds in college contests and every twenty-four seconds in the NBA. An inherent tension between individual creativity and team discipline characterizes basketball. Set plays are important, but a player spontaneously slicing through an alignment of opponents occurs as an instinctive response that blends a coordinated blur of bodily movements with an audacious assault on the hoop. Basketball players seem to defy, or at least to modify, the laws of gravity, juggling the ball from hand to hand and reaching above the rim as easily as those of us bound to the earth raise our arm above our head.

Unlike football movies, films about basketball during the silent era were relatively rare, with a scarcity of productions until the 1970s. The only early feature, *The Fair Co-Ed* (Sam Wood, 1927), deals more with romance than sports, as Marion (Marion Davies) joins a women's college team to attract attention from its coach (Johnny Mack Brown). Another basketball movie, *Campus Confessions* (George Archainbaud, 1938), was released in the late 1930s featuring Betty Grable as a victorious team leader, and two more appeared in the late 1940s: *The Big Fix* (James Flood, 1947), about the attempt to rig games (a similar plot occurs in *The Basketball Fix* [Felix Feist,

1951]), and *Big Town Scandal* (William Thomas, 1948), in which a newspaper editor coaches a team of juvenile delinquents. Two films about the famed Harlem Globetrotters appeared in the 1950s: *The Harlem Globetrotters* (Phil Brown, 1951) and *Go Man Go* (James Wong Howe, 1954). Jane Fonda falls in loves with her college's star player (Anthony Perkins) in *Tall Story* (Joshua Logan, 1960), and Fred MacMurray's invention of Flubber helps his school's team achieve new heights, literally, in *The Absent-Minded Professor* (Robert Stevenson, 1961).

Dramas and comedies dominated the turbulent 1970s. One biographical film, *Maurice* (Daniel Mann, 1973), recalls the tragic injury (on March 12, 1958) to Cincinnati Royals power forward / center Maurice Stokes (Bernie Casey), who became paralyzed after being knocked unconscious during a game with the Lakers, and the extraordinary efforts of his teammate Jack Twyman (Bo Svenson) to care for him. Four dramas deal with coaching: *Mixed Company* (Melville Shavelson, 1974) follows the comic travails of a bigoted NBA coach (Joseph Bologna) persuaded by his wife (Barbara Harris) to adopt ethnically different children; a New York superfan (Gabe Kaplan) seizes the opportunity to coach at a tiny Nevada college in *Fast Break* (Jack Smight, 1979); an Olympic gold medalist (Cathy Lee Crosby) who is mistakenly hired as a high school coach encounters blatant sexism in *Coach* (Bud Townsend, 1978); and a lowly team transforms itself into a winner in *The Fish That Saved Pittsburgh* (Gilbert Moses, 1979)—the latter with appearances by Julius Erving, Meadowlark Lemon, and Kareem Abdul-Jabbar. Two dramas, *Drive, He Said* (Jack Nicholson, 1971) and *One on One* (Lamont Johnson, 1977), involve college players struggling with difficult decisions, the former concerning antiwar sentiments and the latter the callousness of college sports. The most interesting film of the decade, *Cornbread, Earl and Me* (Joseph Manduke, 1975), explores the community's response to the mistaken shooting death of a promising player and the police's subsequent attempt at a cover-up. Finally, *The Great Santini* (Lewis John Carlino, 1979), based on Pat Conroy's novel (1976), explores a highly charged father-son relationship between an abusive Marine Corps pilot (Robert Duvall) and his athletic son (Michael O'Keefe).

As the United States moved into the more conservative 1980s, basketball films almost disappeared from the screen, except those dealing with the reunion of a winning Pennsylvania team in *That Championship Season* (Jason Miller, 1982), a sharpshooting hairy kid in *Teen Wolf* (Rod Daniel, 1985), and the saga of a small-town high school team in *Hoosiers* (David Anspaugh, 1986). This scarcity of basketball movies was reversed by an outpouring in the 1990s, a decade now considered the golden age for these films. Andrew Unterberger suggests that this surge resulted from several factors, including marquee NBA "diva stars" becoming richer and more visible nationally, international stars making the NBA a more global league, popular TV commercials featuring NBA players, and the cross-pollination of hip-hop and basketball. Biopics of Pete Maravich (*The Pistol: The Birth of a Legend* [Frank C. Schroeder, 1991]) and Earl Manigault (*Rebound: The Legend of Earl "The Goat" Manigault* [Eriq La Salle, 1996]) displayed the talents of two different athletes, as did films about Michael Jordan (*Michael Jordan: An American Hero* [Alan Metzer, 1999]) and Dennis Rodman (*Bad as I Wanna Be: The Dennis Rodman Story* [Jean De Segonzac, 1998]), as well as a TV movie about the death of Hank Gathers (*Final Shot: The Hank Gathers Story* [Charles Braverman, 1992]). The more negative aspects of organized basketball also started to appear: illegal pay-offs during the college recruiting process in *Blue Chips* (William Friedkin, 1994) and *He Got Game* (Spike Lee, 1998), outdoor hustling in *White Men Can't Jump* (Ron Shelton, 1992), and drug addiction in *The Basketball Diaries* (Scott Kalvert, 1995), *Heaven Is a Playground* (Randall Fried, 1991), and *Above the Rim* (Jeff Pollack, 1994). Recruiting in a lighter vein finds Kevin Bacon chasing a budding star in Africa (*The Air Up There* [Paul M. Glaser, 1994]) and Billy Crystal an eight-foot man in *My Giant*

(Michael Lehmann, 1998). Women become coaches of men's teams in *Sunset Park* (Steve Gomer, 1996) and *Eddie* (Steve Rash, 1996), a high-jumping dog plays ball in *Air Bud* (Charles Martin Smith, 1997), Michael Jordan cavorts with animated friends in *Space Jam* (Joe Pytka, 1996), and a ghost helps a college teammate in *The Sixth Man* (Randall Miller, 1997).

Following in the tradition of basketball documentaries like *Hoop Dreams* (Steve James, 1994), which traces the lives of two talented inner-city Chicago boys with dreams of professional glory, twenty-first-century basketball programming has been enriched by the advent of the ESPN's *30 for 30* series, an ongoing cycle that has featured stories that range from Len Bias's lethal cocaine overdose (2010) to the University of Michigan's Fab Five (2011) to Magic Johnson's announcement that he is HIV-positive (2012) to a Boston College point-shaving scandal (2014) to a history of my beloved Big East conference (2014) to the firing of coach Bobby Knight (2018). The movies, however, have been far less satisfying than their TV counterparts, a mixed bag of romances jumbled together with athletics (*Love and Basketball* [Gina Price-Bythewood, 2000], *Just Wright* [Sanaa Hamri, 2010]) and comedies (*Like Mike* [John Schultz, 2002], *Juwanna Mann* [Jessie Vaughn, 2002], *Semi-Pro* [Kent Alterman, 2008], *The Hot Flashes* [Susan Seidelman, 2013], and *Thunderstruck*

[John Whitesell, 2012]). More serious subjects, such as a remake of *Othello* called simply *O* (Tim Blake Nelson, 2001) and segregation in *Glory Road* (James Gartner, 2006), seemed to become more a feature of TV documentaries than fiction films. Finally, coaches once again transform losing teams into winners in *A Season on the Brink* (Robert Mandel, 2002), *Crossing the Line* (2002), *Rebound* (Steve Carr, 2005), *Coach Carter* (Thomas Carter, 2005), *Believe in Me* (Robert Collector 2006), *The Mighty Macs* (Tim Chambers, 2009), and *The Winning Season* (Jim Strouse and Graeme Clifford, 2009).

THE COACHES

"They Can Cut the Chains off the Door, but They Can't Make Us Play": *Coach Carter*

The sometimes fraught, sometimes inspiring, relationship between coaches and players often forms the nucleus of the basketball movie. Typical of the hard-ass coach who demands discipline and dedication is *Coach Carter*, a film based on a true story and starring Samuel L. Jackson in the title role. Ken Carter (Jackson) quickly learns that his team at Richmond High School, where he was a star athlete thirty years before, now contains a far different breed of players than common in his era, a recalcitrant group who resent his rules, such as maintaining a passing grade in their schoolwork and dressing properly on game day. Akin to the other coaches discussed in this section, Carter drills his unruly charges in basketball fundamentals during brutal practice sessions. Sweat and dedication pay off in an undefeated season, but Carter locks down the gym until all his players obtain the required grade point average, a principled stance stressing the importance of academics but bitterly opposed by the school board and many people in the community. As he tells the people at the board meeting, "It's the same message that we as a culture send to our professional athletes; and that is that they are above the law. If these boys cannot honor the simple rules of a basketball contract, how long do you think it will be before they're out there breaking the law?" Carter's team, however, responds to his insistence on academic accountability, studying hard to meet his demands. Ultimately, they lose a close game in the state high school playoffs, but the epilogue reveals that several of the players went on to play at the college level, justifying Carter's priorities. Similar kinds of strong-willed coaches appear in films like *Hurricane Season* (Tim Story, 2009), where Al Collins (Forest Whitaker) puts together a makeshift squad in Marrero, Louisiana, following the devastation of Hurricane Katrina, and *Playoff* (Eran Riklis, 2011), about Ralph Klein (Max Stoller), who coaches both the Israeli team and then the West German team into winners of the

European Championships. Such films stress that playing sports is a precursor to adult responsibilities; they underscore the conservative ethos that to be successful in life, even the best athletes, who are usually people of color, must learn to exercise discipline and to accept the rules that govern society.

"A Basketball Hero around Here Is Treated like a God": *Hoosiers*

Hoosiers recounts a classic small-town David versus big-city Goliath story when an undermanned squad from Milan High School (161 students) defeated the far-larger Muncie Central (over 2,000 students)—which had won four previous titles—to capture the Indiana state championship: the so-called Milan Miracle of 1954. In the semifinal round, Milan beat the powerful Crispus Attucks High School (65–52), led by the future NBA star Oscar Robertson. (Betsy Blankenbaker's documentary *Something to Cheer About* (2002) tells the story of the Crispus Attucks Tigers, the first all-Black high school team in the United States to win state titles.) Forty thousand people descended on tiny Milan (population 1,150) to cheer the "Indians" when they returned home from the tournament the next day, and no school near the size of Milan ever won the state tournament again. Director David Anspaugh and screenwriter Angelo Pizzo, fraternity brothers at Indiana University who also paired up to make *Rudy*, dole out generous helpings of nostalgia in their retelling, whisking viewers back to an era before slam dunks shook backboards and when teamwork prevailed over individual flamboyance; as Coach Norman Dale (Gene Hackman) puts it, "Five players on the floor functioning as one single unit. Team, team, team—no one more important than the other." To win, individuals must subordinate themselves to the needs of the team, a willing and mutual conformity necessary to achieve a single goal, a pervasive ideal throughout this genre.

With the film's updating of Frank Capra–like sentiments of triumphant underdogs, *Hoosiers* has remained a very popular film since its release in 1986—and no wonder. It incorporates a virtual compendium of themes interwoven into the fabric of sports movies no matter what game they depict. Most importantly, playing the game properly becomes a second opportunity, and probably a last chance, for most of the major characters. For Coach Dale, whose successful college coaching career ended with a lifetime suspension for hitting a player, it provides the opening to get back into the game he loves, even in the tiny town of Hickory, Indiana. For Shooter (Dennis Hopper), a former player and now the town drunk, it offers a pathway to regain the respect of his son, Everett (David Neidorf), and for his son to reconcile with his father. It gives Myra Fleener (Barbara Hershey), the English teacher, a last shot at love and Cletus (Sheb Wooley), the high school principal, the chance to repay an old friend. Jimmy Chitwood (Maris Valainis), the talented player who has withdrawn into almost total silence due to family traumas, regains his connections with other people. The small, not very athletic, and ridiculed Ollie (Wade Schenck) becomes a last-second-shot hero. Finally, the Huskers' wins generate immense civic pride, evinced in the long procession of trucks and cars, headlights gleaming in the cold midwestern winter nights, that follow the team bus down otherwise-deserted highways from one cramped high school gym to the next—and finally to the big city. *Hoosiers* depicts the blue-collar, disciplined, work-hard ethos that is so prominent in the sports film genre. Yet for all its enfolding of sports conventions, *Hoosiers* offers one major deviation. Set amid the barns and farmlands of Indiana, in a town inhabited mostly by farmers driving dilapidated flatbeds, the movie focuses on the rural, rather than the urban, appeal of the sport. We still hear the slap of the ball and the squeak of sneakers, but this time they echo through cornfields and not city streets.

Because of the film's idyllic trip in the way-back machine, and an all-white team's last-second victory over the racially mixed South Bend Central Bears (whose coach, played by Ray Crow, was the real-life coach of Crispus Attucks High School in 1955), critics such as Deborah Tudor and Alan Nadel have chastised *Hoosiers* as "a retrospective fantasy about a time and place ... that revisits an uncomplicated vision of patriarchal white United States" (Tudor 9), one that "attempts to erase blacks from American history" (Nadel 206); Spike Lee called it simply "racist propaganda" (Leonard, "Heaven" 177). Similarly, David J. Leonard argues that films like *Hoosiers* "not only valorize white masculinity, but ... conceive of a heavenly world of sports defined by both a powerful white (sporting) manhood and the absence of the polluting other (people of color; women)" ("Heaven" 167). Such indictments need to be taken seriously, but they do ignore some basic historical facts, specifically that no Blacks played on the Milan squad and that most of the team's victories came against equally all-white lineups. Of course, *Hoosiers* plays loose with history; this is Hollywood after all. But unlike *Rocky*, a fictional film that consciously promotes a Black-versus-white competition that features an arrogant Black character based on Muhammad Ali, *Hoosiers'* narrative displays a patina of time-period authenticity. One could well argue that ignoring racism during an era when it pervaded all facets of American life was, in and of itself, a naïve and insensitive decision, but such an opinion would eliminate an incredible number of stories located in the past that also never deal with this divisive issue. These objections do, however, raise a persistent, systemic problem among mainstream filmmaking, one that haunts the industry even today: the lack of enough people of color in powerful positions within studios, production companies, and behind the camera to alter the culture of Hollywood and the hidebound belief that white audiences will not spend money to see films about black players. It is blindingly evident that the movie industry must find more avenues of access for artists of color to tell their own stories and those of their own people, not confining them only to these narratives but providing opportunities to explore them.

"This Is More than Just a Game Now": *Glory Road*

In at least one fundamental way, *Glory Road* is the opposite of *Hoosiers*: in this historical re-creation, five Black players from previously unknown Western Texas University (now called the University of Texas at El Paso) trounce the reigning dean of college basketball, Adolph Rupp, and his all-white team from the mighty University of Kentucky to win the 1966 NCAA national championship, shattering southern basketball's segregationist policies. In what has been called the greatest upset in NCAA history and one of the most important games in the history of college basketball, Coach Don Haskins (Josh

Lucas) plays only seven players, all of them Black, ban-
ishing bigoted assumptions that "colored" players were
not intelligent enough and could not sufficiently handle
pressure to win big games. (Following this win, dunking
was banned in the NCAA from 1967 to 1976.) Like *Hoosiers*, the film takes place in a rural setting, "the dusty old
cow town" of El Paso, Texas, but the incorporation of
the dark-skinned Others from Gary, Indiana, Houston,
Detroit, and the South Bronx brings the racism of the era,
and of basketball in particular, into sharp relief, whereas
it was essentially ignored in the earlier movie. Although
Haskins, whose previous job was coaching a girls' high
school team, preaches the same gospel of discipline and
fundamentals in his practices that Coach Dale demands
in *Hoosiers*, telling his players that "showboating is just
insecurity," Bobby Joe Hill (Derek Luke) eventually con-
vinces him to let the Black athletes "play their game," and
the Miners begin beating more prestigious schools. Thus,
Glory Road spotlights fundamental changes to the basic
strategies and playing style that Black athletes inject into
basketball, and Haskins's team represents the transition
from a regimented style of play to a more improvisational
style inspired by the flamboyance of street ball.

While *Hoosiers*, for all its appeal, ignores pervasive
racism, *Glory Road* foregrounds the prejudice evident
during this turbulent era in US history, one referenced in

the film by TV's coverage of the Vietnam War. At times, the team's white and Black players, raw farm boys and hard-bitten city kids with little in their backgrounds to draw them together, blame each other for the problems they encounter on and off the court; ultimately, however, they unite to win the championship against highly favored Kentucky. But such internal disagreements pale in comparison to the hate notes, racial epithets, and violence that escalates as they become nationally ranked contenders. Confederate flags decorate some of the venues in which they play, fans from rival schools bombard the team with trash as they enter the arenas, and some Texas Western alums disagree with Haskins's recruitment policies. In one incident, the team bus pulls into Arlene's Motor Restaurant, and when Shed (Al Shearer) goes to the rest room, three men beat him and stuff his head into the toilet. At another point, Haskins and his wife, Mary (Emily Deschanel), fear for the safety of their young children in this hate-filled environment. Although Rupp had tried to recruit Black players to Kentucky as early as 1964, Haskins's victory over Kentucky proved to be the linchpin that desegregated southern college basketball. In 1997, Don Haskins was inducted into the Naismith Memorial Basketball Hall of Fame, and a decade later, the entire Texas Western team joined their coach there as well.

THE PLAYERS

"Have You Made a Decision Yet?": *He's Got Game*

Director Spike Lee's opening credit sequence in *He's Got Game* (1998) presents a magisterial montage of white and Black kids, young sons and daughters from secluded farmlands to teeming city streets, shooting hoops alone in the backyard or playing together inside fenced courts adjacent to shabby housing projects. Combined, they present a haunting series of strikingly poetic images set to composer Aaron Copland's soaring symphonic piece "John Henry, a Railroad Ballad for Orchestra" (1940, rev. 1952). This skillful blending of sound and image establishes basketball as a quintessentially American game played by diverse athletes from the heartland to the coasts, a sport that possesses the power and beauty of art and that transcends color, time, location, and gender. But the film never dwells on the public face of this sport, ignoring the heroics of desperately heaved, last-second shots or improbable victories before a phalanx of screaming fans; instead, it delves into more personal concerns, exploring the price young athletes inevitably pay for their celebrity. At the heart of Lee's narrative beats an emotionally complex father-son story about Jake (Denzel Washington) and Jesus (Ray Allen—NBA All-Star) Shuttlesworth, with the father being incarcerated in

Attica for accidentally killing his wife (Lonette McKee) and his son being the number-one high school prospect in the country.

Everyone other than Jesus's loving little sister (Zelda Harris) wants to manipulate and exploit him for a promised cash bonanza, including his girlfriend, Lala (Rosario Dawson), his uncle Bubba (Bill Nunn), the gangster Big Time Willie (Roger Guenveur Smith), his high school coach (Arthur J. Nascarella), and potential agents (Al Palagonia and Leonard Roberts) who tempt him with fancy cars and expensive watches. For authenticity, Lee inserts real-life players and coaches who attest to the boy's greatness, including Jim Boeheim, Dean Smith, Roy Williams, John Thompson, Rick Pitino, Bill Walton, Shaquille O'Neal, Reggie Miller, and Michael Jordan. When the Attica warden (Ned Beatty) tells Jake that the governor, a major booster of Big State University, will shorten his time behind bars if Jesus chooses his alma mater, Jake joins the line of eager supplicants trying to influence "the most important decision" in his son's life. Freed for a week to convince Jesus to attend Big State, Jake forms a shaky bond with an abused prostitute, Dakota Burns (Milla Jovovich), while being harassed by two cops (Jim Brown and Joseph Lyle Taylor) sent to keep tabs on him. Lee shows the high stakes of college recruitment during Jesus's visit to Tech U, a potential site for his talents, enduring a sermon by the zealous coach (John Turturro) and participating in a threesome organized by one of his star players (Rick Fox). Finally, his choice comes down to a one-on-one game between father and son that Jesus wins; he banishes his father but still chooses to attend the school that will grant Jake his freedom.

Lee, well-known for his antics while watching his beloved New York Knicks courtside and for his March Madness TV commercials with Samuel Jackson and Charles Barkley, cynically scrutinizes the sordid underbelly of the sport he so dearly loves. As a result, his anger about how the game's purity is squandered in a whirlwind of under-the-table payments, recruiting violations, and financial inducements, as well as how this warped recruiting process harms young Black players, probably doomed the film to box-office failure (budget $25,000,000; US gross $21,554,585). Audiences accustomed to more uplifting, inspirational basketball movies, such as *Hoosiers* and *Glory Road*, ignored a film that fails to indulge in emotional clichés and instead demonstrates an all-consuming greed exhibited even by those who are closest to and most trusted by this talented player. Everyone views Jesus as a commodity, a commercial product that can bring them riches or be discarded if the Coney Island phenom fails in his quest for basketball stardom. *He's Got Game* does, however, offer a partial reconciliation between a redeemable father and an angry son, and perhaps the remorseful antihero of the movie will eventually find peace back with his family. At the same time, even though Jesus signs with the governor's university as a concession to his father, Jake seems unlikely to receive his promised reward because of technicalities, yet another example of how the white power system deceives and takes advantage of Black men.

"I'm a Ball Player": *Love and Basketball*

Similar to *He's Got Game*, *Love and Basketball* initially focuses on the athletic career of two talented high school players, Quincy McCall (Omar Epps) and Monica Wright (Sanaa Lathan), next-door neighbors from their preteen years onward who eventually become a couple. Both Quincy, whose father, Zeke (Dennis Haysbert), was a Los Angeles Clipper player, and Monica, whose mother, Camille (Alfre Woodard), despairs of her daughter's dedication to hoops, end up with full scholarships to the University of Southern California; but after his father's affair destroys their family, Quincy opts for the pros following his freshman season, while Monica stays and becomes a collegiate all-American. Overseas, Monica prospers with a Spanish team but is lonely, while Quincy's diminishing professional career abruptly ends with a torn knee ligament. Two weeks before Quincy's wedding to another woman, Monica reveals that she has been in love with him since they were children and that "the shit won't go away." She challenges him to a one-on-one game, as she puts it, "for your heart," and although she loses the game, Quincy realizes that he still loves her too. In the film's final shot, Monica starts as a point guard in the WNBA, while Quincy sits in the stands holding their baby.

Love and Basketball, one of the few sports films directed by a woman, provides a rare view of the unique dilemmas faced by the female athletes. At home, Monica encounters pressure from her mother, who keeps wishing she would "grow out of this tomboy phase." "I'd rather wear a jersey than an apron," Monica responds. At school, other adolescents make fun of her commitment to athletics as well. In a classic ugly-duckling-turns-into-beautiful-swan scene, Monica shows up at the school's spring dance feminized by her big sister, Lena (Regina Hall), and her rival for Quincy, Shawnee (Gabrielle Union), exclaims, "Damn, girl. I didn't know Nike made dresses." One of the film's most powerful scenes occurs after Monica gives up basketball abroad and discovers that Quincy is engaged. She returns home to find her mother in the kitchen preparing dinner. As their argument escalates, Monica calls her mom "prissy," criticizes her for never standing up for herself, for doing only what her father wanted, and for not attending more than two of her games. Her mother responds that she would "rather bake a pie than shoot a stupid jump-up shot" and that her "female superstar athlete" daughter has always been ashamed because she was "nothing but a housewife." Frustrated and angry by her daughter's condescension, Camille slaps Monica across her face and tells her that she had to put "her dreams on hold" for the good of her husband and children: "My family had three meals a day; they had someone to pick up after them. And when my daughters went to a dance, I could help them get ready. That is what I came to care about." This scene demonstrates how even the people closest to the female athlete, particularly those from a previous generation, often fail to grasp the pivotal role athletics can play in the lives of contemporary women. Even Quincy, who should understand the intense discipline it takes to be an elite athlete, chooses to break up with Monica when she decides to adhere to her coach's curfew regulation rather than listen to him during an emotional crisis. To do what Quincy wants would mean that Monica would not be allowed to play the next game, a penalty she will not risk even for the man she loves.

"You'd Rather Look Good and Lose Rather than Look Bad and Win": *White Men Can't Jump*

The prolific sports-film director Ron Shelton's *White Men Can't Jump* follows the (mis)adventures of a Black and white odd couple of street-ball hustlers in Los Angeles: Sidney Deane (Wesley Snipes) and Billy Hoyle (Woody Harrelson). Billy demonstrates his skill by beating Sidney, and the two form an initially successful partnership to hustle other players, finally winning a two-on-two tournament with a grand prize of $5,000. Even more importantly, the improbable duo triumphs over the legendary street ballers the King (Louis Price) and the Duck (Freeman Williams), winning at the last moment as Billy dunks Sidney's alley-oop pass. The film is notable for its cynical humor and racial byplay, and its dazzling slow-motion shots of both Harrelson and Snipes playing ball (retired pro Bob Lanier was the movie's basketball coach) captures the elevated grace and balletic elegance of the game. In its focus on basketball's outsiders, those who play the game but beyond the boundaries of regulated leagues, *While Men Can't Jump* provides viewers with a cast of characters who hang onto the game as a life raft in a sea of uncertainty and discontent. In *White Men Can't Jump*, money, not trophies or college scholarships, becomes the validation of court skills in the badlands of Los Angeles, and respect accrues to those who earn the right to rule the playground hoops.

BEYOND THE COURT: RACE

Even a cursory analysis of these basketball movies must take into account the complicated issue of race. The 2017 Racial and Gender Report Card from the Institute for Diversity and Ethics in Sports concludes that 74.4 percent of NBA players are Black, while there are only three owners of color (Michael Jordan, Vivek Ranadive, and Marc Lasry, with only Jordan being Black). For comparison's sake, 69.7 percent of NFL players are Black, while there are only two owners of color (Kim Pegula and Shahid Khan, neither of whom is Black). Of Division I basketball teams, 57.2 percent of players are Black, according to the NCAA Participation and Demographics data (Harriot). On the one hand, these statistics might be greeted as good news that reaffirms the cherished belief that sports, at least on the field of play, remain a highly competitive meritocracy, a viable pathway for minorities to obtain the upward mobility, respect, and financial success celebrated in the majority of basketball films. Of course, these films deal mainly with activities on the hardwood, the physical and psychological action that engages viewers. But it behooves us to remember, after those exciting images have drifted into the backyard of our memories, that basketball, like all sports, is a business as well as a game, as moviemaking is a commercial as well as an artistic endeavor. Decisions that are made in the boardroom affect and can even overrule decisions that are made in the locker room: just ask Colin Kaepernick. The sports commentator Bryant Gumbel set off a backlash of outraged criticism when he characterized then NBA commissioner David Stern as "some kind of modern plantation overseer, treating NBA men as if they were his boys" (Golliver), and he has not been the first or the last to make this analogy about the league, although these players are handsomely rewarded for their labors. But clearly the inequities that exist between a league that has been created and sustained by the athletic abilities of mostly Black players and that has only one Black owner of a team cries out for a redistribution of the power structure that controls the professional future of this sport.

3

FOOTBALL MOVIES

> I quickly learned what many Sunday widows already
> realized—that football is not a game but a religion, a
> metaphysical island of fundamental truth in a highly
> verbal, disguised society, a throwback of 30,000 genera-
> tions of anthropological time.
>
> —Arnold J. Mandell, "A Psychiatric Study of
> Professional Football," 1974

"Baseball is what we were. Football is what we have become," observed the *Washington Post* journalist Mary
McGory (Roark 1). Baseball was certainly the United
States' national game from the nineteenth century until
the middle of the twentieth century, but concurrent with
the omnipresence of television in our lives, football then
displaced its older rival as the most popular and lucrative
spectator sport in the country. On October 22, 1939, the
five hundred or so New Yorkers who sat comfortably
at home and watched the Philadelphia Eagles beat the

Brooklyn Dodgers (23–14) on W2XBS—broadcasting from Ebbets Field through the lens of a solitary sideline camera—had no idea that this first entwining of football and television would eventually transform the American cultural landscape. In retrospect, football games seem designed for TV, or perhaps more accurately, television has successfully molded the essential elements of the pro game into prime-time spectacles capable of attracting a massive fan base and churning out huge sums of money. NFL football consistently tops the list of most watched sports programming in the United States. Despite a slide in viewership fueled mostly by a loss of white and younger (eighteen to thirty-four) viewers, NFL games accounted for forty of the fifty (and eight of the top ten) most watched sporting events in 2018, averaging 15.8 million viewers per game; perhaps surprisingly, women favored viewing football over other major sports, accounting for 45 percent of this audience (Hampton). The United States' most watched event almost every year is the Super Bowl. Although its ratings have declined over the past three years—2017 had 111.3 million viewers, 2018 had 103.4 million, and 2019 had 98 million—the cost of a thirty-second commercial for the 2019 game as reported by CNBC still rose to $5.25 million (Schwartz).

The flood of money generated by these figures gushes both ways. In January 2018, Fox agreed to a five-year contract with the NFL that will play the league more than $3 billion, or some $600 million per year—and that was just to broadcast Thursday-night games. Overall, the league made $14 billion in 2017 revenues, and at least twenty-five players (mostly quarterbacks) received annual salaries over $17 million. Commissioner Roger Goodell's stated goal is for the league to make $25 billion by 2027. At this point, NFL revenues derived from media rights now exceed those from ticket sales for game attendance. In a very real and practical sense, then, professional football and TV have maintained an ongoing, extremely lucrative relationship, and the same dispersing of revenues occurs in college athletics as well. In 2016, for example, the 231 NCAA Division I football programs took in an aggregate of $29,635,946, while basketball, a distant second, produced $7,880,290. The average college earned $30 million in football revenues that same year, while college football programs across the country generated more money than the next twenty college sports combined (Gaines).

TV fundamentally shapes how spectators customarily watch and conceptualize football games. When we remember past matches or even visualize fantasy contests, we conjure up images generated by years of watching football on television, no matter the platform. Therefore, movies about this game, as with most other sporting events as well, must necessarily consider the influence and visual construction of television productions, since that medium's aesthetics dominate our viewing of sports. Fans accustomed to seeing football games on television, therefore, instinctively compare what they see at home with what they watch in the theater and, as a result, can summarily reject attempts to portray athletic events that lack the ring of believability—or at least of TV accuracy. Thus, a need to match television's sense of authenticity, often by adopting the visual strategies of these broadcasts, becomes a primary goal, even a necessity, for filmmakers who want their audience to accept the action on the screen as a truthful depiction of reality. Thus, the growing influence of TV aesthetics is clearly evident in the evolution of Hollywood football movies.

That said, it should not be particularly surprising that films about American football follow the same basic trajectory as those about baseball, basketball, and boxing, which in turn employ the conventions, tropes, visual techniques, and narrative arcs of mainstream Hollywood movies as they developed from one era to the next. Looking over the football movies from the early 1920s until the late 1960s, however, one is immediately struck by the overwhelming preponderance of narratives set in colleges. In fact, other than *Triple Threat* (1947), about rival college players who end up on the same pro team, and *Easy Living* (Jacques Tourneur, 1949), about a pro quarterback with a heart condition, no films focus on the professional game until *Paper Lion* (Alex March, 1968), an account of the writer George Plimpton's (Alan Alda) quixotic tryout with the Detroit Lions. This dearth occurred, at least partly, because the professional game was relatively unstable until the late 1930s and even after that period remained far less popular than the college version until the late 1950s, an evolution concomitant with the rise of television and the national excitement generated by the so-called Greatest Game Ever Played—the 1958 championship between the Baltimore Colts and New York Giants. During the 1920s, college football comedies such as *The Freshman* (Fred C. Newmeyer and Sam Taylor, 1925), *The Quarterback* (Fred C. Newmeyer, 1926), *The College Widow* (Archie Mayo, 1927), *So This Is College* (Sam Wood, 1929), and *The Forward Pass* (Edward F. Cline, 1929) and dramas such as *Brown of Harvard* (Jack Conway, 1926), *West Point* (Edward Sedgwick, 1927), *The College Hero* (Walter Lang, 1927), and *Salute* (David Butler,1929) were mainstays.

The same pattern of football movies set on college campuses prevailed over the next three decades as well, with comedies such as *Hold 'Em Yale* (Sidney Lanfield, 1935), *Pigskin Parade* (David Butler, 1936), *The Big Game* (George Nichols Jr. and Edward Killy, 1936), *Father Was a Fullback* (John M. Stahl, 1949), *Bonzo Goes to College* (Fred De Cordova, 1952), and *Trouble along the Way* (Michael Curtiz, 1953) and dramas such as *College Coach* (William A. Wellman, 1933), *Gridiron Flash* (Glenn Tryon, 1934), *Navy's Blue and Gold* (Sam Wood, 1937), *Touchdown Army* (Kurt Neumann, 1938), *The Spirit of Stanford* (Charles Barton, 1942), *Crazylegs* (Francis D. Lyon, 1953), and *All American* (Jesse Hibbs, 1953) playing in theaters across the country. A few musicals (*Maybe It's Love* [William A. Wellman, 1930], *College Humor* [Wesley Ruggles, 1932], *College Rhythm* [Norman Taurog, 1933], and *Good News* [Charles Walters, 1947]) and biographies (of Knute Rockne, Frank Cavanaugh, Jim Thorpe, Tom Harmon, and Elroy Hirsch) primarily set in the same campus environment also entertained audiences. Some of these films featured stars, many in the beginnings of their careers, with roles taken by Harold Lloyd, Joe E. Brown, June Allyson, Dick Powell, Tony Curtis, Bing Crosby, Robert Montgomery, Fred McMurray, Robert Young, James Stewart, Maureen O'Hara, Douglas Fairbanks Jr., and Loretta Young, although none of these performers are remembered for their sports films. Similarly, with the exceptions of William Wellman, Sam Wood, and Michael Curtiz, the directors of these college football films failed to incite much sustained interest either among audiences or scholars.

Of all these lighthearted football comedies, the most enduring is the Marx Brothers' satire of college athletics, *Horse Feathers* (Norman Z. McLeod, 1932). Filled with typical Marxian verbal puns, musical interludes, absurdist actions, and licentious double entendres, the movie seems almost contemporary in its unethical solution for a college's desperate need to mount a successful team: buy good players. Newly installed president Quincy Adams Wagstaff (Groucho) assumes his duties at Huxley College, singing in true professorial fashion about his faculty, "I don't know what they have to say / It makes no difference anyway / Whatever it is, I'm against it." The problem, according to Wagstaff, is Huxley's confused priorities regarding its academic mission: "The trouble is we're neglecting football for an education. . . . Tomorrow we start tearing down the college." For Huxley to beat its traditional rival, Darwin College, Wagstaff recruits what he thinks are two ringers, but this being a Marx Brothers movie, he mistakenly buys an iceman (Chico) and a dog catcher (Harpo) instead of talented professional athletes. Nonetheless, by cheating, Huxley wins the annual Thanksgiving Day contest. Such attitudes strike a very modern note, as recruiting and payoff scandals within NCAA programs continually make headlines. Beneath the antics in *Horse Feathers* lies a critique of the football tail wagging the academic dog, such as is argued more seriously in Gerald Gurney, Donna A. Lopinano, and Andrew Zimbalist's *Unwinding Madness: What Went Wrong with College Sports and How to Fix It* (2017) and Murray Sperber's *Beer and Circus: How Big-Time Colleges Sports Has Crippled Undergraduate Education* (2011), both of which scrutinize the imbalance and tension between college sports and academics.

Hollywood productions took a cynical, raucous turn into the 1960s and '70s, and football movies did as well. Thus, a series of skeptical films explore the more disreputable elements of the game, including *Number One* (Tom Gries, 1969), *The Longest Yard* (Robert Aldrich, 1974), *Semi-Tough* (Michael Ritchie, 1977), *North Dallas Forty* (Ted Kotcheff, 1979), *All the Right Moves* (Michael Chapman, 1983), *Against All Odds* (Taylor Hackford, 1984), and *Everybody's All-American* (Taylor Hackford, 1988). This trend continued into the 1990s, with *School Ties* (Robert Mandel, 1992), *The Program* (David S. Ward, 1993), *Varsity Blues* (Brian Robbins, 1999), and *Any Given Sunday* (Oliver Stone, 1999). Other football films, however, continued the earlier trend of emphasizing the virtues of sports. For example, inspirational biographies of players and coaches who surmount disease and emotional difficulties provide almost a subgenre, such as biographical films centered on Brian Piccolo and Gale Sayers (1971), John Cappelletti, (1977), Rocky Bleier (1980), Bear

Bryant (1984), Ricky Bell (1991), Rudy Ruettiger (1993), Dennis Byrd (1994), Vince Papale (2006), Ernie Davis (2008), Michael Oher (2009), Freddie Steinmark (2015), and Joe Paterno (2018). Most of these films emphasize the courage of players and coaches who, when faced with impediments, summon up the physical and emotional toughness to overcome them. *Paterno* (Barry Levinson, 2018), however, is an exception. An HBO production about the beloved and legendary Penn State coach (played by Al Pacino) who ignored the pedophilic activities of his longtime assistant, it remains one of the few football biographies that demonstrate how an extreme dedication to the game can distort the perspective of a basically good man.

As with movies showcasing other sports, football films provide a conduit for characters to obtain second chances, to correct crucial mistakes, or to live out their dreams of glory: an accidently killed quarterback inhabits the body of a murdered team owner in *Heaven Can Wait* (Warren Beatty and Buck Henry, 1978), a girl leads her high school team in *Quarterback Princess* (Noel Black, 1983), friends replay and revise a devastating high school loss in *The Best of Times* (Roger Spottiswoode, 1986), a woman coaches a boys' team in *Wildcats* (Michael Ritchie, 1986), a small Texas college team beats its big-time rivals in *Necessary Roughness* (Stan Dragoti,

1991), a group of strikebreakers play professional ball in *The Replacements* (Howard Deutch, 2000), an Ohio farmer relives a life-changing game in *Touchback* (Don Handfield, 2012), and a general manager revives the fortunes of the Cleveland Browns in *Draft Day* (Ivan Reitman, 2014). Several films deal with coaches making losing teams or those facing seemingly insurmountable obstacles into winners, such as *Coach of the Year* (Don Medford, 1980), *Little Giants* (Duwayne Dunham, 1994), *Remember the Titans* (Boaz Yakin, 2000), *Friday Night Lights* (Peter Berg, 2004), *We Are Marshall* (McG, 2006), *Gridiron Gang* (Phil Joanou, 2006), *Leatherheads* (George Clooney, 2007), *The 5th Quarter* (Rick Bieber, 2010), and *Woodlawn* (Andrew Erwin, 2015).

THE HIGH SCHOOL FOOTBALL FILM

Although high school football films usually end in the dwindling seconds of important games as desperate teams must score or suffer humiliation, the more important interactions usually transpire before these climactic moments: significant episodes transpire in the relationship between players and their coaches, father figures to their often-wayward sons. At times, as in movies like *All the Right Moves* and *Varsity Blues*, the coach cares far more about his legacy, his winning percentage, than he does about any individual and, as a result, whips his team toward victory with an obsessive single-mindedness that borders on, and sometimes crosses into, sadism. Some of these coaches ignore a player's potentially serious injury and demand that an athlete who should sit out the game instead take the field, insulting his manhood and demeaning his courage in front of teammates unless he accedes to the coach's wishes. Similar to situations found in violent war movies, football films often blur the line between what seems reasonable training for kids about to enter a combat zone, defined by jarring hits and fierce tackles, and what seems to be physical and psychological abuse. What, then, is the essential difference between a marine drill sergeant and a football coach? More crucially, what physical and emotional price is worth high school glory? Many of the football films raise these questions, but their answer has more to do with the scoreboard than with ethical treatment of athletes.

"Being Perfect": *Friday Night Lights*

Based on a nonfiction book by H. G. Bissinger, *Friday Night Lights: A Town, a Team, and a Dream*, about the formidable Permian High School Panthers from Odessa (Texas), and later turned into a critically acclaimed television series (2006–11), *Friday Night Lights* remains a rare football movie that deals as much with defeat, on both the individual and the team levels, as it does with winning. Director Peter Berg shoots the movie in a pseudo-documentary style that often consists of disorienting close-ups and off-kilter angles, compelling us to share these characters' wobbly and uncertain lives; his use of sound effects makes us cringe as we witness the violence on the field and share the emotional distress of the players off it. Early in the film, the team's star running back, Boobie Miles (Derek Luke), suffers a severe knee-ligament tear that ends his season and, most likely, his promising football career. Forced to rely on smaller and less talented team members—particularly quarterback Mike Winchell (Lucas Black) and back/receiver Don Billingsley (Garrett Hedlund)—Coach Gary Gaines (Billy Bob Thornton) must rally his distraught players and face the mounting pressures generated by a town that defines itself by the fortunes of its football team. "Gentlemen," he tells his team, "the hopes and dreams of an entire town are riding on your shoulders. You may never matter again in your life as much as you do right now." These boys see football as a pathway out of dead-end lives in Odessa, but each faces significant challenges. Boobie, who can barely read, wonders how to carve out a life without football and, as a result of his injury, the absence of college scholarship offers. Mike, the sole caregiver for a mother who suffers mental instability, feels cursed and tells Grimes that inside his heart he always feels he is going to lose. The son of a Permian legend who is now a drunken bully (Tim McGraw), Don suffers a daily physical and mental battering from his abusive father. Despite the fact that the coach tells his team that "being perfect is when you can look someone in the eye and know you did not let them down," Grimes, whose salary is larger than the high school principal's, fully understands that "we're in the business of winning": the residents of Odessa expect to win state championships, and if he cannot consistently deliver a title year after year, he will be fired.

In addition to depicting the immense demands on seventeen-year-old kids in an environment that bestows both inappropriate privileges and intense burdens on its athletes, *Friday Light Nights* demonstrates just how quickly their lives can be transformed—and usually not for the better. Older players remember their glory days on the Permian team as the best times in their lives, flaunting their championship rings and admitting that life after high school is just "babies and memories." In a moment of regret and honestly, Don's callous father tells him, "You don't understand. This is the only thing you're ever gonna have. Forever, it carries you forever.... You got one year, one stinking year to make yourself some memories, son. It's all gone after that." But Boobie, who asserts that he is not good at anything else but football, is the film's true sacrificial victim. In the season's first game, with Permian way ahead, Coach Grimes sends in a sub for him, but the kid cannot find his helmet. While the replacement searches, and with only a minute and twenty-one seconds left, Grimes sends in Boobie for a last down, the one that ends his football life. He will try to play again but only do more damage to his unstable knee. In a few ticks of the game clock, Boobie's world falls apart, a causality of bad luck or of chance—a life forever changed due to the accidental misplacement of a helmet. *Friday Night Lights* reminds us about the precariousness of an athlete's life on and off the field. A hero or a goat, a man who captures the American Dream or who, by the slightest swindle of fate, finds himself drowning in a sea of "what coulda beens," the athlete, like one of Shakespeare's tragic heroes, can fall so far into the abyss only because we have lifted him so high.

"That's My Brother": *Remember the Titans*

Similar to Coach Gaines in *Friday Night Lights*, Coach Herman Boone (Denzel Washington) in *Remember the Titans* demands perfection from his team; and he gets it, a perfect season and the state championship. Boone arrives in Alexandria, Virginia, in the racially charged summer of 1971. A white store owner has shot a Black teenager, and despite the resulting friction, the formerly all-Black and all-white schools have been forced to integrate into one high school, TC Williams. Consequently, the town teeters on the verge of exploding into racial violence. To placate the Black community, the Board of Education makes Boone the head coach, a gesture applauded by a minority who have known nothing but "humiliation and despair"; but in taking the place of Bill Yoast (Will Patton), a successful coach with fifteen winning seasons, Boone immediately alienates the white community. The catch, however, is that if Boone loses one game—all the other schools in the conference are all white—he will be fired and replaced by Yoast. Boone inherits a team as racially divided as the town, the whites led by Gerry Bertier (Ryan Hurst) and the Blacks by Julius Campbell (Wood Harris). In an early scene, Boone, reverses the traditional coach/father and player/son dynamic by humiliating his all-American player in front of the entire team: standing inches away from Gerry's face, he forces his best athlete to sanction his authority by demanding, over and over again, "Who's your daddy?" Holding a tough, sometimes brutal, preseason training camp, Boone forces his players to forge bonds with each other, to put the needs of the team above personal animosities. "Nothing tears us apart," the teammates vow, but returning to Alexandra, the volatile world outside the hash marks severely tests their friendships, as do racist members of the community who refuse to embrace tolerance—until the team starts winning.

Remember the Titans, based on a true story, never hides its agenda. It depicts football as a viable pathway toward familiarity, understanding, cooperation, and ultimately alliance against a toxic environment of deep-seated prejudice. Yet again mimicking the combat genre, boys socially conditioned to hate each other learn to look past race and "trust the soul of a man." Over time, the team develops into a melded unit, the group more important than any individual member of it. Perhaps more significantly, the distrustful citizens of a racially divided town band together to laud their winning football team and its coach, another example (as we see repeatedly in the sports genre) of how athletics can transcend social problems, allowing even entrenched bigotry to be subsumed by the frenzied excitement that accompanies athletic success. Teams, as we have seen, come to define physical places whose inhabitants, with little in common, wrap themselves together in a coat stitched by victories. As Gerry tells Julius, "I was afraid of you. I only saw what I was afraid of and now know I was only hating my brother." Ten years later, as the Titans reunite at Gerry's grave, Sheryl Yoast sums up the theme of the movie: "People say that it can't work, Black and white; well, here we make it work, every day. We have our disagreements, of course, but before we reach for hate, always, always, we remember the Titans." Such sentiments strike some people as naïve and sentimental, a simplistic papering over of real-world problems with reel-world fantasies, but sports films consistently reaffirm the power of athletics to inspire change, triumph over adversity, and transcend social inequities.

THE COLLEGE FOOTBALL FILM

"We're Getting Soft": *Knute Rockne All American* and *Rudy*

Notre Dame—adored by its followers, despised by most everyone else—holds an exalted place in US football lore, one due in large part to two films, the classic *Knute Rockne All American* (Lloyd Bacon, 1940) and the more modern *Rudy* (David Anspaugh, 1993), both filmed on the university's campus. Generated by Hollywood's studio system that helped to solidify the conventions of the football movie, the former holds a position among football films similar to that occupied by *Pride of the Yankees* among baseball productions, not to mention that it showcases the most memorable film role of our fortieth president. In fact, *Knute Rockne* blends several types of narratives and techniques together, including the immigrant tale of the United States as a melting pot filled with opportunities, the ample rewards of hard work, the biopic, the talented athlete dying young (see also *Brian's Song* [Buzz Kulik, 1971], *The Express* [Gary Fleder, 2008], and *We Are Marshall* [McG, 2006]), the inclusion of newsreel footage of actual games, cameos by sports personalities, and a perfect marriage with a supportive wife and doting children. Perhaps most importantly, Rockne (Pat O'Brien) provides a spirited and subsequently oft-cited defense of football and its inherent violence as a necessary ingredient of the American character: competitive games are in the nation's best interest, he proclaims before an investigative committee, because they provide a safe outlet for the "natural spirit of combat. . . . The most dangerous thing in American life today is we're getting soft." As is inevitably the case with cinema biopics, the film plays loose with the history, bowing to the demands of drama rather than of facts. The opening scroll sets the tone for the vital role sports play in "molding the spirit of modern America," as Coach Rockne's high standards teach generations of men the ideals of "courage, character, and sportsmanship for all the world."

Unlike the graceful George Gipp (Ronald Reagan), who becomes a star the moment he steps on the gridiron in *Knute Rockne*, Rudy Ruettiger (Sean Astin) epitomizes the narrative of the not particularly talented, white working-class kid who, through intense effort and dedication, achieves his seemingly impossible goal, in this case to play for Notre Dame. (A similar tale on the professional level unfolds in *Invincible* [Ericson Core, 2006], as the thirty-year-old bartender Vince Papale [Mark Wahlberg] secures a spot on the Philadelphia Eagles roster.) Rudy get rewarded not with national headlines or a lucrative pro contract but by experiencing a few glorious minutes on the gridiron and gaining the respect of his teammates. Gipp and Rudy, therefore, represent the extremes of the athletes depicted in the football (and other sports) movies—and how viewers relate to them. Supremely gifted players, like Gayle Sayers and Ernie Davis, represent a level of athletic perfection very few of us can ever hope to achieve. We watch in awe and envy as they juke their way to immortality, despite the tragic events that mar their lives. Others, like Rudy and Vince, become icons of hope for the majority of us struggling to put one damaged foot in front of the other every day, not only in sports but, as Rudy aptly demonstrates, in life as well. If only you work a little harder, if only you try a little more, these movies tell us, you too might just get to realize your wildest dream, even for just a few fleeting moments. Such is the stuff of Hollywood folktales in all its genres but more so in its sports films: the glimmering hope that life is fair, that hard work and good deeds get rewarded, and that every so often we get

our fondest wish granted remains an ingrained component of its mythos.

"As Long as I Keep Making Touchdowns":
Everybody's All-American

Dissimilar from most of the other films mentioned in this
chapter, *Everybody's All-American* has garnered little critical attention or popular acclaim. The reason, I believe,
is because it upends the comforting narratives that traditionally characterize these movies and, in its place,
substitutes a disillusioning portrait of life after football.
The movie begins, for example, not with conventional
images of the hard work and dedication that that we see
in movies such as *Rudy* but with the spectacular feats of
Gavin Grey (Dennis Quaid) at the University of Louisiana in 1956. The fabled "Grey Ghost" appears onscreen
fully formed as a charismatic all-American who marries
his high school sweetheart, Babs Rogers (Jessica Lange),
the school's Magnolia Queen. The glorious, last-second
scoring drive, so prominent in these movies, here occurs
early rather than in the film's final frames. The rest of the
movie chronicles Gavin's downward spiral after these
peak moments, when life off the field proves increasingly
more complex than dashes into the end zone. As such,
Everybody's All-American overtly challenges the inspirational core that endears these films to viewers by showing

that Babs, Narvel Blue (Carl Lumbly), the talented Black player denied a spot on the segregated team, and Cake (Timothy Hutton), Gavin's studious cousin, all fare better economically and emotionally than does their idol as the years slip into decades. Gavin emerges as both the benefactor and the victim of his athletic deeds, forever trapped in his past gridiron fame and forced to revive his glory days for the amusement of sycophantic fans who might provide business opportunities. In one particularly embarrassing scene, he runs onto the field during an old-timer's day game, basking once more in the cheers of the crowd, only to discover they are meant not for him but for the current players. In *Everybody's All-American*, the disgraced, almost pathetic, athlete/hero finally realizes that sports immortality provides flimsy footing for everyday life and that football heroes are only as good as their last touchdown.

THE PROFESSIONAL FOOTBALL FILM

"Can You Win or Lose like a Man?": *Any Given Sunday*

Director Oliver Stone's *Any Given Sunday* begins with a quote from the legendary Green Bay Packers coach Vince Lombardi: a man's "greatest fulfillment" occurs "when he lies exhausted on the field of battle—victorious"—not when he marries, not when he has children, but when, drained to his very bones, he wins. At the professional level, athletes know that it is not just how you play the game but winning the contest that becomes worth any imaginable price, including permanently damaging their bodies by embracing the violence inherent in the sport, subjecting themselves to the dangerous medical measures necessary to keep playing, and even risking permanent paralysis and death. As the brash quarterback Willie Beamen (Jamie Foxx) puts it, "Winning is the only thing I respect." Stone's frenzied, jittery camera movement, replete with disorienting close-ups and slow-motion action, provides audiences with a sense of the speed, the confusion, the intensity, the crunching sound, and the pain that occur when outsized men don battle gear and pound each other into the turf. He also captures the breathless beauty of the perfectly thrown forward pass spiraling gently into the arms of a receiver sprinting downfield. But mostly *Any Given Sunday* confronts the omnipresence of time relentlessly slipping away, as Tony D'Amato (Al Pacino), the beleaguered coach of the Sharks, and his battered quarterback, "Cap" Rooney (Dennis Quaid), face the end of their careers and the emergence of younger men who will take their places, such as Nick Crozier (Aaron Eckhart) and Willie Beamen. Sprinkled into the film are appearances by once-famous NFL players, such as Jim Brown, Lawrence Taylor, Johnny Unitas, Y. A. Tittle, Dick Butkus, and Warren Moon, men whose football careers are now history. As Luther "Shark" Lavay (Lawrence Taylor) tells Willie, "Suddenly, there's no more money, no more women, no more applause, no more dream."

This inescapable sense of the approaching ending, the bittersweet feeling of losing the identity that defined a player for so very long, and the ever-present fear about what happens next sheaths *Any Given Sunday* with a melancholic aura. At the same time, it depicts the extreme dedication and sacrifice demanded to compete at football's highest level. Tony stares longingly at the photo of the family that he has abandoned or that has abandoned him, Cap's wife (Lauren Holly) defiantly refuses to accept that his career is over, and Willie's longtime girlfriend (Lela Rochon) leaves him for a more stable relationship. What a player misses when the game passes him by, Tony tells Willie, is the team, the camaraderie of the "other guys looking back at him in the huddle, those eleven guys seeing things the same way, all of them looking downfield together." Constant references are made to how football imitates life, such as in Tony's locker-room speech: "Life's this game of inches, so is football. Because in either game—life or football—the margin for error is so small. One half a step too late or too early, and you don't quite make it. . . . Those inches, that's gonna make the fucking difference between winning and losing, between living and dying!" As such, *Any Given Sunday* emphasizes how football games both "give and take away." Sports at their heart, then, are about more than winning; they bond men together, forcing each of them to go beyond what they thought was possible and to labor together to achieve a difficult, painful common goal as long as the game might last.

From high school to college to the NFL, football has emerged as the dominant sport in American culture. For some people, this rise to prominence represents the accentuation of a pernicious cult of masculinity (the so-called warrior male) defined by violence; simultaneously, the verifiable dangers to the health of the sport's participants makes football the prime villain for those who revile what they characterize as the overemphasis of sports in academic institutions and everyday life. "Football players, like prostitutes," observed the actor Merle Kessler, "are in the business of ruining their bodies for the pleasure of strangers" (Quote Garden). In the movie *Concussion* (2015), for example, the Nigerian pathologist Dr. Bennet Omalu (Will Smith) faces opposition from the NFL when his research demonstrates that the serious blows to the head received by football players can result in chronic traumatic encephalopathy (CTE), a condition that leads to mental deterioration. Although some of the football movies incorporate such critiques, most emphasize football's ability to mold the character of young men, to teach them both how to lead and how to work together. They often demonstrate that the building of strong bodies accustoms athletes to hard work and, through diligent effort, simultaneously builds disciplined minds and passionate spirits. Many sports movies, including football films, offer viewers nostalgic fulfillment, a chance to rectify past mistakes, as well as characters who become role models by achieving a seemingly impossible goal despite numerous obstacles. As such, they become an intricate part of the American Dream, repeatedly demonstrating that sports transcend their fields of play, their lines of demarcation, and become an ongoing metaphor for life.

4

BOXING MOVIES

"The Sweet Science of Bruising" celebrates the physicality of men even as it dramatizes the limitations, sometimes tragic, more often poignant, of the physical. . . .
Boxing is for men, and is about men, and *is* men. A celebration of the lost religion of masculinity all the more
trenchant for its being lost.

　　　　　　　　　　　　　—Joyce Carol Oates, *On Boxing*

The tradition of literary works featuring boxing stretches
as far back as Homer's book 23 of the *Iliad* (762 BC),
where he describes boxing as one of the eight events at
the funeral games of Patroclus, to Pindar's *Seventh Olym-
pian Ode* (464 BC) in praise of Diagoras of Rhodes, the
most famous boxer in antiquity, and to the boxing match
between the Trojan Dares and the Sicilian Entellus in
book 5 of the Roman poet Virgil's *Aeneid* (20 BC); the
sport even receives a passing mention in 1 Corinthians

9:25–27: "I do not fight like a boxer beating the air." Over the course of history, authors referencing boxing in their works include some of the greatest names in English literature, such as Daniel Defoe, William Hazlitt, Jonathan Swift, Lord Byron, Henry Fielding, Arthur Conan Doyle (Sherlock Holmes was an amateur boxer), and Alexander Pope, as well as Americans such as Langston Hughes, Sherwood Anderson, Maya Angelou, Ernest Hemingway, Norman Mailer, Jack London, Richard Wright, H. L. Mencken, and James Baldwin—including singer-songwriters Warren Zevon ("Boom Boom Mancini"), Paul Simon ("The Boxer"), and Bob Dylan ("Hurricane"). Joyce Carol Oates claims that boxing is a silent spectacle and that "lacking a language it requires others to define it, celebrate it, complete it" (50). Perhaps writers also see a connection between themselves, battling alone against the blank page or silent screen and ultimately facing the verdict of a judgmental public, and the nearly naked pugilist facing his challenger in the ring, although the verbal jabs of critics surely sting less than the punches of trained professionals—at least physically.

As these artistic works establish, boxing is the oldest of the four sports discussed in this book, and evidence of its existence, in one form or another, has been found in the earliest civilizations: carvings in Samaria made in the third century BC, hieroglyphic sculptures in Egypt from around 1350 BC, and boxing gloves depicted in a Minoan fresco from around 1600 BC. Boxing events in which competitors wrapped their hands in leather thongs were included in the ancient Olympics as well, making their debut in the twenty-third Olympiad in 688 BC. In England, the first official bout was recorded in 1681, with bare-knuckle fights continuing until one of the prizefighters could no longer stand. The year 1867 saw the publication of a set of regulations, "The Marquis of Queensberry Rules," that modified and modernized the sport with changes such as fighting within a specified ring (twenty-four feet square), padded gloves, three-minute rounds, use of only the hands, and the ten-second count for a fighter knocked down. Boxing became an Olympic sport in the St. Louis games of 1904, and its subsequent popularity across the United States provided an ongoing gateway for immigrants to obtain status and wealth. Black fighters, however, were not allowed to contend for the heavyweight championship until 1908, when Jack Johnson beat Tommy Burns. Jewish fighters, like Barney Ross, and Italians, like Rocky Marciano, became celebrated representatives of their ethnic groups, and in 1937, Joe Louis emerged as a powerful symbol for the American Black community when he captured the heavyweight championship, as did Muhammad Ali during the Vietnam era.

The boxer stands apart from the other athletes discussed throughout this book, as does his (and sometimes her) sport. All four sports contain varying levels of violence, but boxing remains the only one whose overt goal is to physically demolish the other competitor and, as such, has the distinction of being "America's most popularly despised sport" (Oates 187). This warrior's one and only goal is to subdue the man who stands in front of him, to knock him to the canvas so hard that he cannot rise within ten seconds. Scoring points or runs or baskets matters not, only cathartic knockouts. The boxer is the archetypal working-man athlete whose trade compels him to earn a livelihood within his hands. He swings no bat, dribbles no ball, catches no pass—nothing but his reflexes and his hands deflect his opponent's punches. Standing alone and half naked in the center of the spotlit ring, this modern heir to the gladiatorial tradition faces a foe desperately bent on destroying him. No pads cushion the blows to his body. No helmet protects his face and head from getting battered. Punch or be punched. Destroy or be destroyed. Teammates who would share the struggle with him simply do not exist; substitutes cannot be summoned from the bench to replace him should he falter. Where once he danced around the ring taunting his rivals with the snap of his jab or vanquishing them with the power of his uppercut, now he fends off blows and clings to his tormentor for a momentary respite from pain. The boxer's body bears witness to his history and his suffering; it "carries the reminders of every glove that laid him down or cut him" (Paul Simon, "The Boxer"). It is the source of his pride, of his power, and ultimately of his betrayal. For the body will inevitably betray him. It will get injured, it will grow frail, and it will turn old. Once the envy of both male and female spectators, he will come to know his body's limitations and that it always contained the seeds of his fate. Like Oedipus, the boxer finally discovers that the culprit navigating the path to his destiny lies not in the ring but, rather, within himself.

As boxing matches connect modern athletes with their ancient ancestors, so prizefighting films are our oldest sports movies and have endured as a source of popular entertainment from the silent days to our modern era of multiplexes: "No art has shaped our perception of the boxer as much as has motion pictures" (Grindon 3). Boxing offers a viable setting, a cast of recognizable characters, and an intrinsic dramatic structure that seems ready-made for movies, and over time, directors and cinematographers have discovered inventive ways to capture these decisive moments, both inside and outside the ring. Every generation of filmmakers who produce boxing matches strives to establish an authenticity of sight and sound; but as the art of cinematography developed, moviemakers began to see the advantages of manipulating time and space as well, predominantly through creative editing. Crafting exciting montages of the action, they speed up the cuts between images so that viewers have a subjective sense of how it would feel if they were actually present at the match. Ongoing technical innovations such as lighter-weight cameras and more flexible recording devices allowed filmmakers far more freedom to experiment with their visual constructions, fashioning thrilling re-creations of boxing matches as well as inspiring compilations of images showing fighters training for their big bout. For example, Rocky Balboa's growing strength as depicted in his training regimen and famous run through the chilly morning Philadelphia streets, combined with evocative music, provides viewers with a stirring preamble to his epic fight with Apollo Creed.

Restricted by heavy and bulky cameras, early filmmakers gravitated toward shooting boxing matches not only because of their popularity but also because they provided a far easier setting, the relatively small and stable ring, that allowed them to capture the ebb and flow of the event. Dan Streible demonstrates that over one hundred prizefight films were produced from 1894 to 1915, far more than of any other sport, and shows how four specific types of boxing films characterize this era: (1) fictional narratives; (2) reenactments (or faked) versions of real bouts;

(3) exhibitions; and (4) recordings of actual prizefights (236). Edison's lab became the site where several famous fighters sparred for a few rounds in front of the camera, with the resulting pictures sold around the country as peephole movies in Kinetoscope locations. Because boxing films could potentially reach far more spectators than those attending an actual fight, Progressive Era reformers continually attacked them as immoral models for the era's youth and fought to have them banned. Later in the century, when Jack Johnson became heavyweight champ—a fact that contradicted widely held, racist beliefs in the inherent superiority of the white race—their protests took on a bigoted tone, as the recorded films of his fights were either suppressed or banned in various states "as part of a tendency to control the social aspirations of black citizens" (Streible 249).

Compared to the history of movies about other sports, boxing has attracted the best overall roster of first-rate directors, including David O. Russell, Ron Howard, Robert Rossen, Elia Kazan, Martin Ritt, Michael Curtiz, Robert Wise, Jim Sheridan, Franco Zeffirelli, Walter Hill, Clint Eastwood, Martin Scorsese, John Huston, Norman Jewison, and Michael Mann, among others. As a result, it should not be a surprise that there are more outstanding boxing films than those of any other sport. In *Knockout: The Boxer and Boxing in American Cinema*, Leger Grindon traces the historical trajectory of boxing movies from the silent days onward. He sees their evolution in the following cycles and clusters, including some representative examples:

1. The Depression cycle (1931–33): *The Champ* (King Vidor, 1931), *Winner Take All* (Roy Del Ruth, 1932)

2. The Popular Front cycle (1937–42): *Kid Galahad* (Michael Curtiz, 1937), *The Crowd Roars* (Richard Thorpe, 1938)

3. The noir cycle (1946–51): *Body and Soul* (Robert Rossen, 1947), *Champion* (Mark Robson, 1949)

4. The "after the ring" cycle (1950–56): *The Quiet Man* (John Ford, 1952), *On the Waterfront* (Elia Kazan, 1954)

5. The racial and ethnic prejudice cycle (1950–54): *Right Cross* (John Sturges, 1950), *The Joe Louis Story* (Robert Gordon, 1953)

6. The failed hybrid cluster (1956–57): *Somebody Up There Likes Me* (Robert Wise, 1956), *The Harder They Fall* (Mark Robson, 1956)

7. The comeback cycle (1975–80): *Rocky* (John G. Avildsen, 1976), *Raging Bull* (Marin Scorsese, 1980)

8. The African American documentary cluster (1993–2005): *When We Were Kings* (Leon Gast, 1996), *Ali* (Michael Mann, 2001)

9. The masculinity crisis / postmodern cycle (1993–
    2005): *Girlfight* (Karyn Kusama, 2004), *Million Dollar
    Baby* (Clint Eastwood, 2004)

Among these evolutionary cycles and clusters, Grindon
specifies the six dramatic conflicts that form the foundation of the boxing-movie narrative: body and soul or
material versus spiritual values; a critique of the success
ethic; the opportunity to enter mainstream society versus
loyalty to the boxer's ethnic/immigrant community; a
masculinity crisis that involves a romance; anger at injustice; stoic discipline in the face of life's cruelty (7).

We should not forget, however, that the so-called
Golden Age of boxing (the 1920s and 1930s) was dom-
inated by white fighters and champions, such as Jack
Dempsey, Jack Sharkey, Gene Tunney, Max Baer, and
James Braddock, many of whom refused to fight Black
boxers; no Black fighters were allowed to contend for
the heavyweight championship from the time that Jess
Willard beat Jack Johnson in 1915 until Joe Louis won
the crown in 1937. A film of the 1910 bout in which Jack
Johnson knocked out the former heavyweight champion
James Jeffries, who stated that he felt obligated to return
to the ring "to reclaim the heavyweight championship
for the white race, . . . to demonstrate that a white man
is king of them all" (Orbach 297), was banned in many

states. (For more on Johnson, see Ken Burns's two-part documentary, *Unforgivable Blackness: The Rise and Fall of Jack Johnson* [2004].) These facts led to an overarching irony: the majority of films about boxers, as well as most of the films discussed in this chapter, are about white athletes, although Black boxers (and Hispanic fighters) have dominated the sport for a very long time. The most recent exceptions to this industry practice are the two *Creed* movies (Ryan Coogler, 2015 / Steven Caple Jr., 2018). *Ali* (Michael Mann, 2001) and *The Hurricane* (Norman Jewison, 1999) were the most important films about Black fighters before these films. During roughly this same period, boxing movies about white fighters included *The Boxer* (Jim Sheridan, 1997), *Million Dollar Baby* (Clint Eastwood, 2004), *Fighting Tommy Riley* (Eddie O'Flaherty, 2004), *Cinderella Man* (Ron Howard, 2005), *Rocky Balboa* (Sylvester Stallone, 2006), *The Fighter* (David O. Russell, 2010), *Grudge Match* (Peter Segal, 2013), *Southpaw* (Antoine Fuqua, 2015), *Bleed for This* (Ben Younger, 2016), *The Bleeder* (Philippe Falardeau, 2017), *Journeyman* (Paddy Considine, 2018), and even more. Such a disproportionate number of films about white rather than Black boxers is probably due to the continuing belief that white audiences will not attend films starring and about Black people, a remnant of conventional wisdom that should be discarded in the wake of the record profits garnered by *Black Panther* and *Creed.*

"Prizefighting Is an Insult to a Man's Soul": *Golden Boy*

Based on Clifford Odets's play (turned into a 1964 Broadway musical starring Sammy Davis Jr.), *Golden Boy* (Rouben Mamoulian, 1939) follows Joe Bonaparte (William Holden), an Italian fighter forced to choose between a promising career as a violinist or a quick-money livelihood as a pugilist. His father (Lee J. Cobb) encourages him to continue his pursuit of music, but his manager, Tom Moody (Adolphe Menjou), a menacing gangster, Eddie Fuseli (Joseph Calleia), and a tough woman he falls for, Lorna Moon (Barbara Stanwyck), all manipulate him to remain in the ring, particularly as he beats his way toward the championship. For them, Joe is a money-making machine, a commodity in which they have invested and from whom they seek to reap substantial dividends; as such, they divvy up "pieces" of him as if he were composed of detachable parts. Indeed, Fuseli continually refers to him in the third person, never addressing him directly with personal pronouns or by his first name, even when Joe stands right in front of him. "Music and fighting don't mix," Joe tells Lorna, as he fears that his hands, soaked in brine for over a year, can never again play the violin. Ultimately, he discards music for fast money, symbolized by a new car. But after Joe kills a Black fighter nicknamed Chocolate Drop (Jimmy "Cannonball" Green) in the ring, his whirlwind of guilt eventually drives him to reject a big-payday championship match and return to his supportive family. "I've come home," he says in the film's last lines, entering into a loving embrace with Papa and, we assume, to once again play the music.

The film contains many of the settings and characters that would remain consistent in boxing movies: the sweaty gym filled with aspiring fighters, the packed and often smoky arena, the threatening gangster, the faithful trainer, the greedy manager, the ten-second knockout count, the fight montage, the values differences between generations, the untrustworthy girlfriend, the lack of a mother figure, the connection between sons and their fathers, the immigrant's desire for social acceptance and financial rewards, and the hangers-on who seek to capitalize on the boxer's fame. In *Golden Boy*, however, the conflict between music and fighting becomes one between creativity and competition, a shaking off of the emotions and sensitivity in a man's nature in favor of his more violent instincts. Joe truly loves music, but he fights for money, recognition, and respect; he wants people "to know who he is" and fears that a career in music will provide neither the fame nor the fortune that will win

Lorna's love. While Joe's home life is depicted as a happy and loving environment filled with laughter and music, outside this safe and stable cocoon he expresses an angry volatility that finds an outlet only in the ring, becoming a fighter fueled "with hate, not heart."

"Fight for Something, Not Money": *Body and Soul*

Body and Soul remains one of the most underappreciated sports film in the US cinema. The story follows the trajectory of Charlie Davis (John Garfield), a tough and arrogant boxer who, with the help of his girlfriend (Lilli Palmer), ultimately redeems himself by defying the command of his devious gangster/manager (Lloyd Gough) to fix his final bout. The movie shines a spotlight on both the glamorous world of fashionable restaurants and fancy parties open to celebrated athletes and the seedy side of the sport in poolrooms, card games, and gambling dens. Technically, the film employs stylish noir compositions that heighten its sense of physical danger and psychological distortion, and its documentary-like depiction of the fight sequences provides viewers with a sense of authenticity never achieved in previous movies. To put the viewer into the ring with the fighters, cinematographer James Wong Howe (who had been a boxer) mounted handheld cameras on his shoulder and roller-skated around the ring as the action progressed, thus showing the final bout from Charlie's sometimes-blurry viewpoint. His inventive strategy was so effective that, according to various newspaper accounts, audience members stood and cheered as Charlie fought his way to a title bout.

As is Joe Bonaparte in *Golden Boy*, Charlie is the product of a working-class, ethnic community, this time a Jewish neighborhood on the Lower East Side rather than an Italian enclave. In fact, Charlie demonstrates what Joe might have become if he did not give up fighting. Joe's father is the major factor in his home life, but Charlie's mother (Anne Revere) dominates his domestic world. Both parents uphold a solid and moral standard that their sons first ignore but ultimately come to accept as the right path for their futures. In the theatrically released version of *Body and Soul*, however, some of the Jewish elements were eliminated, such as a neighbor telling the family, "In Europe, Nazis are killing people like us just because of our religion, but here Charlie Davis is champ"—a reaffirmation of the United States as a free country of tolerance, of laws, and of opportunities. Charlie never mentions his religion, and his beloved mother, who wants her boy to get an education rather than pursue a career in fighting, never objects when he brings home the obviously non-Jewish Peg (Lilli Palmer). But one of the reasons the neighborhood idol decides to win rather than throw his last fight is because of the shame and guilt he feels after he learns that the Jewish community has bet heavily on him. "Fight for something, not money," Charlie's mother tells him, and by the end of the movie, he follows her admonition.

One of the most significant aspects of *Body and Soul* is Charlie's relationship with Ben Chaplin (Canada Lee), an ex-champ whom Charlie nearly kills on his way to the top. Ben, the prototype of the physically damaged former champion present in many boxing films, functions as a tragic prophecy for the current title holder of his potential future. Ben serves as a father figure, role model, moral standard, and blatant warning to the younger fighter; the two minority-group members square off against the businessmen/racketeers who see Charlie only as a money-making commodity and whose illegitimate payoffs corrupt their sport. Ben brings into focus the exploitation of ex-fighters, and by extension Blacks and other minority have-nots, by the powerful men who rule society with muscle and money, an indictment of a defective US capitalist system that values financial gain over everything else. Thus, Ben evolves into the ethical center of the film. His death, a dynamic lesson in courage, helps to inspire Charlie to save his "soul" by fighting fairly in the ring. After Charlie rallies to win his last fight, he spits out Ben's brave words to the frustrated gangster: "What you gonna do, kill me? Everybody dies!" As a result, Ben emerges as a bold, proud, and dignified man, one of the most positive portrayals of Black characters to emerge from Hollywood during this era.

WOMEN FIGHTERS

Joyce Carol Oates maintains that "Boxing is a purely masculine activity and it inhabits a purely masculine world. . . . Men fighting men to determine worth (i.e. masculinity) excludes women as completely as the female experience of childbirth excludes men. . . . [Boxing] is a distillation of the masculine world, empty of women" (70, 74). In the following two films, however, women invade the formerly hermetically sealed world of professional boxing; as a result, their disruptive appearance as combatants adds unique elements to the evocation of masculinity and the empowerment of women in these movies, similar to when so-called kick-ass women who are unafraid to fight appear in the action and superhero genres. For example, rather than occupying more conventional roles as mothers or girlfriends who either offer support or provide distractions (including both love and sex) for the men at the center of the narrative, these female fighters challenge cultural stereotypes, embody a different kind of physicality, redefine beauty, and offer a more competitive sexuality. That said, however, both of these movies incorporate some of the traditional rags-to-riches conventions seen as far back as classic movies like *Golden Boy* and *Body and Soul*. The complicated relationship of the fighter to her family and community and boxing as a viable passageway for marginalized members of society to gain respect and financial rewards both play a prominent role in these movies, as does the lack of sex in both movies. But placing a woman into the ring, a sacred space previously occupied only by men, alters the fundamental dynamic of these boxing movies and, even while incorporating traditional themes, makes them relevant to contemporary cultural issues.

"Tough Ain't Enough": *Million Dollar Baby*

Director Clint Eastwood's *Million Dollar Baby* (2004)—nominated for seven Oscars and a winner of four: for best director, actress, supporting actor, and picture—contains a melodrama surrounded by the harsh and often-crooked world of professional boxing. The elderly Frankie Dunn (Eastwood), a former cut man and manager, now trains contenders in his gym, the Hit Pit, where his longtime friend Eddie "Scrap-Iron" Dupris (Morgan Freeman), an ex-boxer with only one functional eye, works and lives. The men share an often-sarcastic give-and-take rapport with each other, but they clearly care about and depend on each other. For unclear reasons, Frankie remains estranged from his daughter, Katie, who returns his letters without ever opening them. Into their lives comes Maggie Fitzgerald (Hilary Swank), a self-described white-trash waitress from "the scratchy-ass Ozark town of Theodosia, . . . somewhere between nowhere and good-bye," who desperately wants Frankie to train her. At first reluctant ("I don't train girls!"), the crusty Frankie admires Maggie's work ethic and sees her potential, so he finally agrees to become her trainer/manger; in about a year, he takes her up the ladder of contenders and eventually secures her a million-dollar match for the middleweight crown. On Maggie's way to winning the championship bout, her opponent blindsides her with a vicious punch after the bell, sending her crashing into a corner stool and causing a spinal injury that permanently paralyzes her from the neck down. Bedridden, unable to breathe without mechanical aids, and eventually forced to have her gangrenous leg amputated, Maggie asks Frankie to end her life, and after much soul-searching, he complies. Although movie boxers die from injuries suffered in the ring, and a goodly number of fighters end up defeated and punch drunk in these films, main characters usually deliver the lethal blow, not receive it; as a result, *Million Dollar Baby* offers a distinct variation on this formula.

For Maggie, whose father died far too early and whose rapacious family scorns her achievements, and for Frankie, who has lost the love of his daughter, the bond between boxer and trainer/manager evolves into a loving relationship that provides each with a substitute for the persons they most miss in their lives. In essence, along with Scrap, they form a pseudo-family not based on blood but rather on a shared goal and mutual admiration for each other's talents, a common theme in Eastwood's movies. "Boxing is about respect," says Scrap in the voice-over, "getting it yourself and taking it away from the other guy." Maggie yearns for respect and sees boxing as the only way to avoid "scraping dishes and waitressing, ... going back home, finding a used trailer, buying a deep fryer and some Oreos." Frankie, who attends Mass almost every day for twenty-three years, intuitively understands that taking care of Maggie might be the only way he can forgive himself for the transgression (and we never know what this is) that compelled his child to so utterly reject him. Although Frankie is unable to express his feelings for Maggie directly, he buys her a robe with the Gaelic phrase "Mo Cuishle" (my darling / my blood) stitched on the back, which becomes her nickname. "The magic of fighting," Scrap says, is that it is a "dream nobody sees but you." In *Million Dollar Baby*, Frankie and Maggie share the same dream for a time before it disintegrates into a nightmare. As David Desser notes, in *Million Dollar Baby*, Eastwood "isn't interested in gender parity between male and female fighters; he is interested in myth, religion, and redemption" (161).

"I Didn't Make the Cheerleading Team": *Girlfight*

Maggie Fitzgerald in *Million Dollar Baby* and Diana Guzman (Michelle Rodriguez) in *Girlfight* could be sisters in arms. Both struggle to overcome the financial hardships of their close-to- poverty-level existence ("where you can be raped in your own fucking stairway," as Diana puts it) and to rise above the dead-end lives of their families: Maggie from the backwoods of Theodosia, Missouri, and Diana from the Red Hook housing projects in Brooklyn. Each mourns the loss of a dead parent—Maggie's father and Diana's mother—while their remaining parent ridicules their love of boxing and demeans their hard work. Maggie finds Frankie, and Diana finds Hector (Jaime Tirelli), father figures who appreciate their athletic talents and guide them through the minefield of professional bouts. Both women feel at home in the sweat-drenched gym and spend countless hours trying to learn how to box properly, usually after male fighters have quit for the day. Each film, therefore, contains extensive training montages showing the main character's steady growth from a clumsy amateur to a more polished professional boxer. More importantly, Maggie has learned to funnel her aggression and keep it inside the ring, swathing her belligerence with a courteous and restrained blanket that muffles her temper. Younger and less under control, Diana rarely gets through the day without erupting into a shouting match or physically beating up someone, be it a schoolmate, her father, or just anyone who has annoyed her. When she finally channels her hostility into her matches, the blows inflicted by opponents stoke the furnace of her anger, turning her ever-smoldering rage into a bonfire. Her head dips down a bit, her eyes narrow into slits, the skin seems to tighten on her cheeks, and her face resembles a half-human/half-not-so-human being ready to wreak destruction on its prey. It is a less extreme version of Bruce Banner turning into the Hulk, without the shift in size and green overlay, and both transformations culminate in hurt foes.

"The equality crap has gone too far," complains the manager (Victory Sierra) of Diana's boyfriend, Adrian (Santiago Douglas), when Diana and Adrian are forced to face off against each other in the ring. As is almost always the case in movies focusing on female athletes, Diana encounters almost continual sexism, humiliation, and distrust as she barges headfirst into a world usually reserved only for men. Interestingly, her brother, Tiny (Ray Santiago), faces the reverse of Diana's discrimination when he opts for a field that his father considers unmanly: painting. As a result, the film engages with gender stereotypes that prove, within the contours of the narrative, to be nothing but artificially constructed categories that stifle individual desires and creativity. Men and women cannot fight each other in the ring, says Hector, "because girls don't have the same power as boys," a claim that hits the canvas along with Diana's male adversaries. Director Karyn Kusama films the actual fights, particularly the final one against the conflicted Adrian, with a skillful blend of slow-motion, point-of-view shots that lock the viewer into the position of the character receiving, and sometimes reeling from, the punches. Such a claustrophobic tightening of the frame engenders a feeling of constraint and entrapment, while a shaky, handheld camera technique endows these scenes with a documentary quality that adds to the film's authenticity.

"Eat Lightning and Crap Thunder": Rocky

In 2011, Sylvester Stallone, along with Mike Tyson and Julio Cesar Chavez, was inducted into the International Boxing Hall of Fame. Each year during this august ceremony, Bill Conti's stirring theme from Rocky welcomes the newest members to join the Hall's exclusive club, one reserved for the sport's greatest practitioners; that year, the man who conceived of and then personified a fictional boxer took his place among men who had actually fought in the ring—and for good reason. Despite the film's relatively small ($1 million) budget, lack of recognizable stars, and cramped twenty-eight-day shooting schedule, *Rocky* originally grossed some $117,235,145 (adjusted gross for ticket price inflation is $505,065,400) and gave birth to the most popular and financially successful sports-movie franchise (grossing over $1.4 billion) in cinema history, with *Creed II* adding to those robust figures. *Rocky* received ten Academy Award nominations, taking home Oscars for best director, best film editing, and best picture. Forty some years after the movie's initial release, buses still park at the bottom of the seventy-two stone steps leading to the entrance of the Philadelphia Museum of Art, discharging gaggles of tourists from all over the world who gleefully mimic the boxer's joyous sprint up and exuberant dance atop those now-famous steps, raising their arms above their heads and no doubt humming Conti's "Gonna Fly Now." The site of a fictional movie has become as much of an attraction as the cracked Liberty Bell. Certainly, the movie's rags-to-riches story of a lovable lug who gets the chance of a lifetime to fight for the heavyweight championship, who finds a shy ugly duckling beneath a pair of oversized glasses who turns into a swan, and who is tutored into becoming a "dangerous man" in just five weeks by a crusty old trainer struck a resonant chord during the United States' bicentennial celebration. Like that last sentence, the film is a virtual compendium of boxing-movie clichés and conventional characters, but its tender story of two social outcasts falling in love, its evocation of Philadelphia's rough and dilapidated neighborhoods, and its inspiring narrative of an engaging underdog who just wants "to go the distance" remains an appealing blend of style and sentiment to this day. The film opens with a flourish of trumpets and a fresco of Jesus holding the Eucharist and a chalice set above a seedy boxing-clubhouse ring in which two fighters alternately slug and hug each other, an appropriately blended image for a film about a boxer's resurrection and redemption.

Neither resurrection nor redemption, however, is much on the mind of critics such as Frank Tomasulo who contend that Rocky's battle with Apollo Creed (Carl Weathers), a brash and boastful character based on Muhammad Ali, represents an example of "submerged racism." For them, the film demonstrates white manhood desperately reasserting itself, an ominous indication of a sizable cultural shift back to the conservative values that dominated a seemingly more stable past in the United States' history, one whose conformist principles would replace the chaotic breakdown of traditions during the 1960s and early 1970s: "For those who felt that affirmative action policies and the athletic accomplishments of African Americans went against the grain of traditional values, Rocky Balboa, the 'great white hope,' represented an avatar of the racial divide in America. . . . The film's endorsement of self-reliant white individualism appealed to those disturbed by the radical visions of the early counterculture. At its core, *Rocky* wallows in white lower-class resentment over Black economic gains in a time of recession" (Tomasulo 162). In retrospect, such an analysis has some foundation given the cultural reversal that culminated in the United States' turn rightward, Ronald Reagan's election to the presidency, and Hollywood's retreat from the intellectually aggressive filmmaking that highlighted its output during the previous ten years or so. But *Rocky*'s style is far from a throwback to earlier eras of moviemaking, particularly its on-location authenticity and use of cinematographer Garrett Brown's new technology via the Steadicam. More to the point, who is the villain in *Rocky*? Is it the bout promoter or the petty gangster, prime suspects in early boxing movies? Perhaps a better question might be, Is there even a villain in *Rocky*? Later sequels provide Rocky with the frightening opponents Clubber Lang (Mr. T), Ivan Drago (Dolph Lundgren), and Thunderlips (Hulk Hogan). Clubber might be cast into this racist paradigm, but Apollo Creed does not fit within the same sinister mold. Apollo's major sin is to underestimate Rocky, and his crucial mistake is to value his business interests over his training schedule. In fact, until the fight begins, Paulie (Burt Young) threatens Rocky and his own sister, Adrian (Talia Shire), more violently than does the heavyweight champion of the world. In the bout itself, Apollo, after taunting Rocky in the early rounds, proves worthy of respect, battling the surprisingly strong challenger despite sustaining serious injuries. *Rocky* clearly reverses the traditional economic status evident in boxing movies by making the Black athlete financially successful and the white fighter struggling to pay his bills, and there is certainly some level of wish fulfillment by having a white fighter of little renowned (based on Chuck Wepner's fifteen-round slugfest with Muhammad Ali, one of only four times Ali was knocked down in the ring) take a far-superior boxer to the limits of his talent.

The year that *Rocky* won the best picture Oscar, it beat out films about a corrupt president, an immoral television industry, and a man driven mad by a rotting society, and the film remains surprisingly affecting. One remembers the boxing match between Apollo and Rocky, the shot of Adrian between the bars of the birdcage in the pet store, Rocky's workout in Pauli's meat locker, Apollo's theatrical entrance dressed first as George Washington crossing the Delaware and then as Uncle Sam, and of course the training sequence that culminates in the run up the stone steps. But seeing it again, I am struck by the little touches that add humanity to Rocky's character, his refusal to break a guy's thumb for the loan shark, his walking of the teenage girl home through the rough neighborhood despite her disdain for his moralistic lecture, his staring into the mirror and wondering how the young boy in the photograph turned out to be such a disappointment to himself, and his self-doubt the night before the big fight. For all its clichés and familiar characters, the film allows us to see the softer side of a tough man who just wants to prove that he is "no bum." As such, it remains a quint-essential boxing film and one of the most beloved sports movies in the history of the US cinema.

"It Defeats Its Own Purpose": *Raging Bull*

In the upper-left-hand corner of the frame, hemmed in by the ropes of the ring as if they were the bars of a cell, a lone fighter dressed in his warm-up robe shad-owboxes in slow motion. The film's title appears in red between the top two ropes in the center of the hazy, black-and-white image that resembles a 1940s newsreel or a 1950s TV program. The boxer dips and sways, deliv-ering right- and left-hand blows into the air, the bottom of his robe swirling around his legs as if caught in a mild breeze. Flashbulbs explode in the background, while on the soundtrack Pietro Mascagni's haunting "Cavalleria

Rusticanao: Intermezzo" (part of his one-act opera, it denotes the passage of time) adds an aura of classical grace to the jabs and uppercuts. As the credits continue, the boxer turns to face us; still throwing punches, he moves closer to the camera but stays crowded on the left side of the frame, as if he could slip out of our sight at any moment. But, then, he turns his back to us and struts back and forth alongside the rope like a restless, caged animal. Later, we discover that this is Jake LaMotta (Robert De Niro) fighting his most powerful and enduring opponent: himself.

This is the first of many images that linger in the viewer's mind long after the theater lights return us to our daily lives: Jake pouring ice water down his shorts to refrain from having sex with Vicki (Cathy Moriarty); Vicki's legs dangling in the pool when Jake first meets her; Sugar Ray Robinson (Johnny Barnes) delivering the blow that will end Jake's boxing career; Jake's corner man rinsing him off with a combination of water and blood; Jake punching Vicki in the face and fighting with his brother, Joey (Joe Pesci); Joey slamming the car door on Salvy (Frank Vincent); the long unbroken traveling shots that follow LaMotta from the locker room into the ring as the Steadicam rises from eye level to above the ring without a cut; blood dripping off the ropes of the ring; De Niro's startling weight transformation from the buff LaMotta to the paunchy LaMotta to the obese LaMotta, a sixty-pound shift; Jake in jail furiously pounding his fists and his head against the wall in frustration. And then there are the fights, each shot with one camera mainly inside the ring and deftly choreographed to a specific rhythm, like a dance number in a musical, except for the blows, the blood, and the brutality. Scorsese lit flames under the camera, so the environment has a smoky look, and used the voice of the original announcers who broadcast LaMotta's bouts for authenticity. But listen carefully to the soundtrack for how Frank Warner, the sound effects supervising editor, fills it with screeching and howling animal sounds. Even more impressively, Scorsese uses silence to emphasize a significant moment. That first image during the title sequence makes us aware of watching the work of a brilliant visual artist, and the rest of the movie demonstrates that we have witnessed a modern classic. Indeed, among the film's many honors (which includes Oscars for De Niro and editor Thelma Schoonmaker) *Raging Bull* was voted the best film of the 1980s by many critics and ranked fourth on the American Film Institute's 10th Anniversary List of the 100 Greatest American Films of All Time.

All that duly noted, *Raging Bull* is not an easy movie to watch, and De Niro's LaMotta inspires a jumble of emotions. Inside the ring, he displays courage, strength, and tenacity. After being pulverized by Sugar Ray, for example, the dazed fighter staggers over to his conqueror and brags, "You never got me down." (The real LaMotta never hit the canvas in any of his fights.) Outside the ring, he is uncouth and uncontrollable, truly a raging bull who eventually takes a dive at the behest of powerful gangsters. He orders his wives around and beats them when they refuse to kowtow to his demands. In particular, Jake constantly dreads that Vicki is cheating on him, perhaps because he is cheating on her. Paradoxically, then, this epitome of manhood who fears no one inside the ring becomes a fixated, insecure man outside the ring, neurotically terrified that his wife is having sex with other men, including his brother. He accuses her of thinking about other men while having sex with him, and in their worst fight, Vicki screams that she has "sucked the cock" of all their friends and says of one of them that "his fucking cock is bigger" than Jake's. As she hits his most vulnerable insecurities, Jake knocks her out and leaves her lying on the floor. Scorsese shows Jake staring at himself in the mirror throughout the film, trying to figure out who he is and, more importantly, what he has become.

More than films about other sports, boxing movies tend to have layers of meaning that incorporate issues other than the sport itself. The viscerally enthralling depictions of fight scenes, of course, are indispensable to the voyeuristic appeal of these movies; but the iconic figure of the isolated boxer, as differentiated from the shared experiences of baseball, football, or basketball teammates, joins US cinema's lineup of lone heroes, those rugged individuals who gallantly battle against an array of powerful social forces stacked against them. Thus, the boxer who fights for respect and dignity stands on a platform beside the laconic cowboy and the heroic soldier in the pantheon of mythic cultural figures propagated by Hollywood cinema. The fact that he usually comes from a working-class community—and if successful abandons that environment—allows the boxing movie to explore issues of race and class, as well as the stark economic disparities that characterize US society. In fact, because most boxing movies examine the struggles of economically disadvantaged members of society, they could fit rather easily into the genre commonly labeled the "social problem" film. Paradoxically, then, boxing movies both reinforce and undermine conventional narratives that invoke the American Dream; they demonstrate how a determined athlete can surmount most any obstacle but also that these barriers of race, class, economics, and gender severely limit opportunities for blue-collar citizens who strive to achieve a better life for themselves and their families. While real figures offer inspiring examples of determined characters beating the odds inside and outside the ring, what remains unspoken is that most of the time in the real world, the odds beat the man.

Boxing movies are as much about the fighter's internal battles as they are about his external bouts. Spectators both recoil from and embrace the ritualistic punishment that the men in the ring sustain, but on some level the hail of blows strike one as metaphorical as well as literal, the rite of passage, the necessary suffering, for the boxer to reach a new level of understanding about himself. Narratively, these films inexorably build toward the climatic fight between the protagonist and his most significant opponent, not only a physical contest between fierce competitors but also an externalization of the boxer's struggle between conflicting parts of his psyche. As many commentators have noted, the central figure's antagonist is often an embodiment of his darkest traits and fears, a doppelganger who threatens to destroy his world. Thus, the battle that frames the action and separates it from the rest of society inside the ring becomes an extremely physical event in which pain will inevitably occur, but it is also a psychological pilgrimage where redemption and regeneration can transpire: a series of three-minute rounds that will determine the course of the rest of his life.

In addition to the socioeconomic and psychological contexts of boxing movies, they are inherently about masculinity as well, given that they foreground the fighter's sacrificed and battered body. The other three sports in this book have no weight requirements, no set categories solely determined by the body of the athlete. But in boxing, whom you fight literally results from how many pounds you carry, the size of the body being the crucial factor. As evident in many of the films mentioned in this chapter, boxing movies tend to juxtapose the professional world of the boxer with the personal space dominated by women and families. The characters in these films inhabit mostly gyms, training camps, and rings, men-only settings that remove their main character from the domestic comforts, and conflicts, of hearth and home. These professional settings provide environments for men to be with other men, exiling women and the opportunities for romance and the trouble that they beget. Remember: "women weaken legs"—and the mind of the fighter as well. Although female boxers appear in a few modern movies, they are continually measured against their male counterparts, and like the environments occupied by men, their world is demarcated by the masculine conventions that compose the world of boxing. In some of these films, the women function simply as a way to scrutinize the psyche of the men surrounding them, much as Black characters in movies often exist to explore various aspects of their white counterparts. Basically, therefore, the more a woman acts like a man, the better her chance for victory in the ring.

CONCLUSION
Fields of Perpetual Dreams

> For many years the conviction has grown upon me that civilization arises and unfolds in and as play. . . . All play means something.
>
> —Johan Huizinga, *Homo Ludens: A Study of the Play-Element in Culture* (1938)

Millions upon millions of people experience great enjoyment and ongoing gratification from participating in, watching, and supporting the athletic culture that pervades American (and worldwide) society. Yet such passionate and intense involvement often impedes sports enthusiasts from considering thorny questions that make spectatorship a more complicated activity than just plopping down on the couch, flicking on ESPN, and cheering for your team. Admittedly, a deeper knowledge of issues beyond the fields of perpetual dreams can interfere with the enjoyment of watching a contest. Knowing, for example, that a 2017 research study of dead former National League Football players revealed that 110 out of 111 of

them showed evidence of chronic traumatic encephalopathy (neurological damage) resulting from their playing
days makes watching NFL football something of a guilty
pleasure. Yet a narrow focus only on individual games or
players that excludes a consideration of broader questions of cultural ramifications and ideological assumptions ignores the profound and pervasive impact of
sports across the globe. While acknowledging the spectrum of pleasures that sports provides, a discussion of
complex and often-controversial issues can lead to better
understanding our deep commitment and communal
fixation with athletes and their competitions, as well as
their significant role within our society. The sociologist
Jay Coakley, for example, has developed what he calls
"The Great Sports Myth," which explores the widely held
conviction that athletics positively influence society, and
examines the revered status of sports globally: "We've
developed this sense that sport is beyond reproach. If
there are any problems associated with sport, it has to be
due to bad apples that are involved in it, who are somehow incorrigible enough that they can't learn the lessons
that sport teaches, so we have to get rid of them. That fits
into American culture as a whole, and our emphasis on
individualism, personal choice and individual responsi-
bility" (qtd. in Barth 2). Through such a multidisciplinary
lens, the scholars cited throughout this book, along with

many others, scrutinize how Americans conceptualize athletic competitions. Their thought and questions add indispensable layers to an overall awareness of the culture of sports in the United States. To that end, "anyone who wishes to understand sport needs to understand the economic and political forces shaping and reshaping contemporary sporting experiences" (Boyle and Haynes 222). In many cases, these scholarly analyses challenge the formidable hold of heavily vested commercial interests that doggedly resist confronting, much less investigating, dominant assumptions about the role, function, and power of athletics. In some cases, they can also lead to changes in the sport itself, to how we perceive athletes, and to the ways athletic competitions are presented on the screen.

In the spirit of an examination that raises issues that it cannot resolve, let us begin with some basic assertions and then move on to a brief consideration of three fundamental issues that, hopefully, will lead you to more extended discussions beyond the limitations of this book. All sport competitions are a test. Whether it be of physical skills, such as running, hitting, throwing, or catching, or those more elusive character traits of spirit, confidence, heart, and intelligence, someone wins and someone loses. These athletic contests call on participants to give their best, despite knowing that winning—like so many things in life—sometimes depends as much on luck or chance or fate as it does on the skills of the participants. Because athletic contests have champions and also-rans, the movies about sports often become as much about failure as they are about triumph. In fact, a common convention in the genre revolves around how an athlete builds on failure to succeed, echoing the words of Michael Jordan from a Nike ad: "I've missed more than nine thousand shots in my career. I've lost almost three hundred games. Twenty-six times, I've been trusted to take the game-winning shot and missed. I've failed over and over and over again in my life. And that is why I succeed." But a combination of the right event, the perfect performance, and the precise moment in time can allow an athlete to transcend the limitations of the playing field and evolve into something far larger than a singular presence, such as the representative of a country, the incarnation of a cultural issue, or the embodiment of a particular historical era. Think of Jessie Owens shattering Hitler's declaration of Aryan superiority during the 1936 Olympics, of the US hockey team's shocking the heavily favored Russians in the 1980 Winter Olympics, or of Colin Kaepernick kneeling during the national anthem to protest police brutality and racial injustice. That said, however, sports—and consequently the movies that depict them—are rife with contradictions.

"HOW MUCH CAN YOU KNOW ABOUT YOURSELF IF YOU'VE NEVER BEEN IN A FIGHT?": VIOLENCE

Other than in sports, where in society do we condone, indeed excessively praise and highly reward, the violence we cheer and the agony we pay exorbitant fees to witness in athletic contests? Bloodshed is in the DNA of athletics, pain is the essential component, and red is the defining color. The ferocious nature of these sports, even experienced secondhand and stylized in films, draws some audience members to movies about athletics, and watching an athlete's screen surrogate violate social taboos against violence helps make these movies so popular. To that end, Jennings Bryant writes about how watching sports (and I would include sports movies) and identifying with a sports hero provide the spectator with an "ideal means to assert power and dominance by siding with a sports hero who asserts control via legitimized play" (281). In an interview with the Brazilian magazine *Vega*, Steven Spielberg put it succinctly when he said, "In movies, violence is filmed with perfect illumination, spectacular scenery, and in slow motion, making it even romantic. However, in the news the public has a much better perception of how horrible violence can be and it is used with objectives that do not exist in the movies." Often our attention is riveted on one athlete, and the wounds endured earn our admiration and assure us of the competitor's worthiness to reap rewards. Recall that *agon*, the ancient Greek word for a struggle or athletic contest, is also the root of *agony*, and sports are as much about suffering as about victory; in fact, most film narratives demonstrate that victory can be validated and achieved only after an athlete endures a substantial amount of pain and torment to justify it. Pain in sport is not only valuable but essential, and an athlete's ability to tolerate it and still compete distinguishes him or her from lesser citizens. Thus, the pain that results from punishing the body and the manner in which the athlete accepts suffering as a necessary rite of passage remain fundamental elements in the appeal of sports and movies about them. What, then, are the ramifications, social and personal, of the violence that is so much a part of some popular sports?

"EVER TRIED. EVER FAILED. NO MATTER. TRY AGAIN. FAIL AGAIN. FAIL BETTER.": MASCULINITY

Athletes, and consequently sports movies, provide young men with dramatic versions of masculinity, as well as concrete examples of how a man should react when faced with physical and psychological adversity. These graphic images exert a powerful influence and often become an important conscious or subconscious component of male identity. Michael Messner, for example, argues that sports play a significant role in developing masculine personalities: "Young males are predisposed to define their masculinity through their achievements rather than their intimate relations with others. Boys develop gender identities with social institutions, which are themselves products of gender relations" (*Power* 43). As a result, athletic events and sports movies have always been crucial ingredients in the social crucible that forges concepts of masculinity in US culture. Athletics and sports movies—the so-called New Jock Cinema—create, disseminate, and reaffirm an idealized and aggressive masculine identity defined primarily through intense competition, physical action, and psychological toughness. But this is a hotly contested image of manhood. Critics call this construction of masculinity "a collective fiction, a strikingly narrow and archaic model . . . providing dramatic symbolic proof of the natural superiority of men over women" (Messner, *Out* xi, 93), while supporters note that sporting competitions have historically been acknowledged to inculcate courage and strength in young men, as well as to "build character, instill discipline, develop competitive instincts, improve physical and mental fitness, [and] encourage religious and patriotic sensibilities" (Crosson 69). What, then, are the positive and negative components of manhood evinced in athletes and their competitions?

Every sport is based on the skillful execution of bodily movements. Looking at the finely sculptured bodies of athletes, whether the viewer is a male or a female, remains a pleasurable act that adds to the visual and erotic lure of sports that converts athletes "to a commodity, the mediatised object of collective fantasy or desire" (Chaudhuri 1765). Books by Susan Cahn, Thomas Scanlon, and Allen Guttmann all examine the eroticism inherent in sports that make a spectacle of and glorify the exceptional body. A cadre of scholars have studied the body as a site of meaning or, more theoretically, a "contested ideological terrain" ripe for extended scrutiny (Messner, *Out* 31). Ironically, as Messner notes, "the athlete is viewed as an icon of health, but the reality is that the high-level athlete's body is constructed through processes that are often very unhealthy" (*Out* 5). In addition, and paradoxically, sporting competitions and sports movies inevitably contain examples of the physical limitations of the body and the seeds of its inevitable destruction. Some, like boxing matches, are almost entirely based on destroying another man's body. While we are watching these bodily icons of manhood perform athletic feats, therefore, we simultaneously witness their breakdown through the injurious effects of game. Exposing the body, no matter how fit, to the brutal training regimens that lead up to athletic events and then to the consistent punishment leveled on the field of play cannot help but weaken, and ultimately diminish, the very bodies we have been conditioned to admire for their discipline, strength, beauty, and toughness. What, then, are the personal and cultural effects of the masculinity celebrated in athletic competitions and sports movies?

"I HAVE LEARNED THAT I REMAIN BLACK IN A WHITE WORLD": RACIAL ISSUES

Movies continue to play a significant role in the elevation of athletes to a very high rung on our cultural ladder. But commentators such as Deborah Tudor argue that many Black athletes, in particular, despite their overwhelming participation in sports on almost every level, discover that "this particular American dream is a dead end": "Black children who focus all their attention on athletics risk academic failure, and the odds against becoming another Michael Jordan are overwhelming. . . . Fastening all their hopes on sports as an escape deflects children from other career paths. The myth of upward mobility through athletics provides an unrealistic model for success, and so it becomes part of a mechanism which bars black children from more realistic goals. . . . The percentage of athletes who make it from the playgrounds to the professional leagues is small" (3). Consider the broader implications of Tudor's assertion. This same sentiment might well be expressed, in one form or another, for any student, Black or white, who desperately wants to enter equally competitive fields with discouraging odds for success, say music or drama or any of the arts. Should we advise the promising high school violinist to stop practicing hour upon hour and instead spend that time studying for the LSATs? Is it fair and reasonable, therefore, to discourage disenfranchised kids from dedicating themselves to sports because their chances of obtaining a spot on a professional roster are so slim? A majority of the sports films that appear on our movie screens incorporate as their major thematic statement the belief that personal dedication, commitment, and discipline can surmount most any obstacle, including racism, and thereby lead to athletic success and financial rewards. What, then, is the socially responsible, as well as realistic, advice that should be given to young athletes of color, and is it different from the advice given to young white athletes?

Several scholars who deal with issues of race emphasize the inequities between how white and Black athletes are often presented in the media, including films. David J. Leonard, for example, argues that white privilege dominates our conception of and response to athletes: "Public sporting discourse not only celebrates white intelligence as unique and exceptional, but also praises the character that white athletes bring into contemporary sporting cultures. In a sporting world in which black athletes routinely face criticism about their attitude, style of play, or lack of love for the game, white athletes are celebrated as different, as conveyers of fresh values who can redeem sports, save it, and make it great again" (*Playing* 10). Such critiques repeatedly point out that white athletes are lauded for their intelligence and work ethic, while Black athletes are praised for their natural ability and physical feats. It was not so long ago, for example, that common wisdom dictated that a Black man was not intelligent enough to play quarterback. For these scholars, sports film that mythologize the "white (often working class) Everyman"—such as *Hoosiers, Cinderella Man, Miracle on Ice, Invincible, The Natural,* and so many more—function as conservative political allegories that reaffirm white privilege and thereby become a "regressive site of white masculinism" (Babington 9). Indeed, whatever emotional appeal these films possess may well stem from this nostalgic (some might say racist) portrayal of their white protagonists' embodiment of the positive traits conventionally idealized in sports movies. What, then, is the role of race in sports, both on and off the field of play and in the depiction of athletic contests?

A FEW PARTING WORDS

One could argue that the four sports discussed in this book bear a rough resemblance to musical styles and groupings. Together, they offer distinctive variations of rhythm, pitch, dynamics, and texture that speak to us on a level beyond words. American sports, American cinema, the American Dream: certainly not a holy trinity but one that feeds our communal hunger for heroes and ideals, our primordial craving for myths and folktales. Real and fictional sports figures embody the American Dream, and US cinema recycles their stories in films that span the decades, providing testaments to the belief that the dream is not a myth but an achievable objective. After all, Lou Gehrig became a big-league star, and the T. C. Williams Titans overcame racism to go undefeated. Jimmy Chitwood hit the last shot for the Hickory team, and Rocky went the distance with Apollo Creed. Consciously, we realize that Gehrig actually did play for the Yankees and that Rocky sprang from the mind of Sylvester Stallone, but on some deeper level, little distinguishes them from each other. Movies have enabled these men and teams to elbow their way into the American Dream and, as representatives of its enduring power, have helped to perpetuate its hold over our imagination.

ACKNOWLEDGMENTS

Thanks to Sara Greenleaf, Dan Mulvey, and Jennifer Nance at the Hobart and William Smith Colleges Library; Jared Case and Sophia Lorent at the George Eastman Museum; Gwendolyn Audrey Foster and Wheeler Winston Dixon, series editors of the Quick Takes series; Leslie Mitchner, Nicole Solano, and Andrew Katz at Rutgers University Press; and Rae-Ellen Kavey and Marc Friedman, generous family members.

FURTHER READING

Agyemang, Kwame J. A. "Managing Celebrity via Impression Management on Social Network Sites." *Sport, Business and Management: An international Journal* 6.4 (2016): 440–59.

Andrews, David L., and Steven J. Jackson, eds. *Sport Stars: The Cultural Politics of Sporting Celebrity*. New York: Routledge, 2001.

Baker, Aaron. "Sports Films, History, and Identity." *Journal of Sport History* 25.2 (1998): 217–33.

Baker, Aaron, and Todd Boyd. *Out of Bounds: Sports, Media, and the Politics of Identity*. Bloomington: Indiana UP, 1997.

Barnes, Simon. *The Meaning of Sport*. London: Short Books, 2006.

Bell, E., and D. Campbell. "For the Love of Money." *The Observer* 23 May 1999.

Bonnet, Valerie. "Sports in Films: Symbolism versus Verismo; A France–United States Comparative Analysis." *InMedia: The French Journal of Media Studies* 6 (2017): 1–32.

Boyle, Raymond. "Television Sports in the Age of Screens and Content." *Television and New Media* 6 (Apr. 2014).

Briley, Ron, Michael K. Schoenecke, and Deborah A. Carmichael, eds. *All-Stars and Movie Stars: Sports in Film and History*. Lexington: U of Kentucky P, 2008.

Bryant, Howard. "How Did Our Sports Get So Divisive?" *New York Times* 12 May 2018.

Carlson, Brad D., and D. Todd Donavan. "Human Brands in Sport: Athlete Brand Personality and Identification." *Journal of Sport Management* 27 (2013): 193–206.

Carmody, Tom. "Mobile Is Changing How We Are Watching Sports. Here's How Verizon Is Leading the Charge." *Adweek* 20 Feb. 2018.

Carrington, Ben "Introduction: Sport Matters." *Ethnic and Racial Studies* 35.6 (2012): 961–70.

Cave, Andrew, and Alex Miller. "Mobile Technologies and Social Media Are Transforming Sports and Sports Business." *The Telegraph* 23 June 2015.

Curtiss, Ellen T., and Susan Eustis. "Youth Team, League, and Tournament Sports: Market Shares, Strategies, and Forecasts, Worldwide, 2018–2024." *WinterGreen Research* 1 Sept. 2018.

Durbin, Daniel, and Yann Descamps. "The Politics of Discourse on the Fields of Dreams: Political Messaging and the Mediated Representation of Sports." *InMedia: The French Journal of Media Studies* 6 (2017).

Dyck, Noel, ed. *Games, Sports and Cultures*. Berg, 2000.

Dyson, Michael Eric. "Athletes Have Always Led the Way." *New York Times* 22 Oct. 2017.

Eastman, Susan Tyler, and Andrew C. Billings. "Biased Voices of Sports: Racial and Gender Stereotyping in

College Basketball Announcing." *Howard Journal of Communication* 12 (2001): 183–201.

Fausto-Sterling, Anne. *Sexing the Body: Gender Politics and the Construction of Sexuality*. New York: Basic Books, 2000.

Ferrucci, Patrick, Edson C. Tandoc Jr., Chad E. Painter, and Glenn Leshner. "A Black and White Game: Racial Stereotypes in Baseball." *Howard Journal of Communications* 24 (2013): 309–25.

Fox, John. *The Ball: Discovering the Object of the Game*. New York: HarperCollins, 2012.

Gau, Li-Shiue, and Jeffrey D. James. "An Empirical Exploration of Relationships between Personal Values and Spectator Sport Consumption." *International Journal of Sport Management, Recreation, and Tourism* 16 (2014): 37–55.

Harvey, Marc, and Lawrence J. Babich. *Sports Films: A Complete Reference*. Jefferson, NC: McFarland, 1987.

Jarvie, Grant, with James Thornton. *Sport, Culture and Society*. 2nd ed. New York: Routledge, 2012.

Jhally, Sut. "Cultural Studies and the Sport/Media Complex." *Media, Sports, and Society*. Ed. Lawrence A. Wenner. Newbury Park, CA: Sage, 1989. 70–93.

Johnson, Victoria. "Together We Make Football: The NFL's 'Feminine' Discourses." *Popular Communication: The International Journal of Media and Culture* 14.1 (2016): 12–20.

Jones, Glen. "In Praise of an 'Invisible Genre'? An Ambivalent Look at the Fictional Sports Feature Film." *Sport in Society* 11.2–3 (2008): 117–29.

Kang, Jay Caspian. "If Sports Betting Is Legalized, Could Its Hunger for Analytics Restore an Older, Purer Version of Fandom?" *New York Times* 25 Apr. 2017.

Lieberman, Viridiana. *Sports Heroines on Film: A Critical Study of Cinema Women Athletes, Coaches and Owners.* Jefferson, NC: McFarland, 2004.

McCallum, Jack. "Reel Sports Hollywood Trends Come and Go, but Sports Movies—Clichéd, Corny, Sometimes Downright Comical—Are Never Out of Fashion. Just Don't Call Them Sports Movies." *Sports Illustrated* 5 Feb. 2001: 97–102.

McChesney, Robert W. "Media Made Sport: A History of Sports Coverage in the United States." *Media, Sports, and Society.* Ed. Lawrence A. Wenner. Newbury Park, CA: Sage, 1989. 49–69.

Meng, Matthew D., Constantino Stavros, and Kate Westberg. "Engaging Fans through Social Media: Implications for Team Identification." *Sport Business and Management: An International Journal* 5.3 (2015): 199–217.

Miller, Andrew C. "The American Dream Goes to College: The Cinematic Student Athletes of College Football." *Journal of Popular Culture* 43.6 (2010): 1222–41.

Nielsen Sports. "Unified Measurement Defining a New Sponsorship Currency." 1 June 2017. Web.

Pearson, Demetrius W., et al. "Sport Films: Social Dimensions over Time, 1930–1995." *Journal of Sport and Social Issues* 72.2 (2003): 145–61.

Poulton, Emma, and Martin Roderick, eds. *Sport in Film.* New York: Routledge, 2008.

Reed, Heather L. *Introduction to the Philosophy of Sport.* Lanham, MD: Rowman and Littlefield, 2012.

Reiss, Steven A. "Sports and the Redefinition of American Middle-class Masculinity." *International Journal of the History of Sport* 8.1 (1991): 5–27.

Rowe, David. "If You Film It, Will They Come?" *Journal of Sport and Social Issues* 22.4 (1998): 350–59.

Sutton, W. A., et al. "Creating and Fostering Fan Identification in Professional Sports." *Sports Marking Quarterly* 6.1 (1997): 1–22.

Vogan, Travis. *Keepers of the Flame: NFL Films and the Rise of Sports Media.* Urbana: U of Illinois P, 2014

Wenner, Lawrence A., ed. *Media, Sports, and Society.* Newbury Park, CA: Sage, 1989.

Whannel, Gary. "Winning and Losing Respect: Narratives of Identity in Sport Films." *Sport in Society* 11.2–3 (2008): 195–208.

Young, Diane. "Fighting Oneself: The Embodied Subject and Films about Sports." *Sport in Society* 20.7 (2017): 816–32.

Zelinsky, William. *Nation into State: The Shifting Foundations of American Nationalism.* Chapel Hill: U of North Carolina P, 1988.

WORKS CITED

Babington, Bruce. *The Sports Film: Games People Play*. London: Wallflower, 2014.

Baker, Aaron. *Contesting Identities: Sports in American Film*. Urbana: University of Illinois Press, 2003.

Barth, Brian J. "Stadiums and Other Sacred Cows." *Nautilus* 39 (18 Aug. 2016).

Benjamin, Walter. "The Work of Art in the Age of Mechanical Reproduction." *Illuminations*. Trans. Harry Zohn. New York: Schocken Books, 1968. 217–51.

Bissinger, H. G. *Friday Night Lights: A Town, a Team, and a Dream*. 25th anniversary ed. Boston: Da Capo, 2015.

Bordo, Susan. *The Male Body: A New Look at Men in Public and in Private*. New York: Farrar, Straus and Giroux, 1999.

Boyle, Richard, and Richard Haynes. *Power Play: Sport, the Media and Popular Culture*. Harlow, UK: Pearson/Longman, 2000.

Bryant, Jennings. "Viewers Enjoyment of Televised Sports Violence." *Media, Sports, and Society*. Ed. Lawrence A. Wenner. Newbury Park, CA: Sage, 1989. 270–89.

Cahn, Susan K. *Coming on Strong: Gender and Sexuality in Women's Sport*. Urbana: U of Illinois P, 2015.

Chaudhuri, Supriya. "In the Ring: Gender, Spectatorship, and the Body." *International Journal of the History of Sport* 29.12 (2012): 1759–73.

Collignon, Hervé, Nicolas Sultan, and Clément Santander. *The Sports Market: Major Trends and Challenges in an Industry Full of Passion*. Chicago: ATKerney, 2011. Web.

Crosson, Sean. *Sport and Film*. New York: Routledge, 2013.

Desser, David. "I Know I'm Blind as a Slab of Concrete, but I'm Not Helpless: The Aging Action Hero." *Tough Ain't Enough: New Perspectives on the Films of Clint Eastwood*. Ed. Lester Friedman and David Desser. New Brunswick, NJ: Rutgers UP, 2018. 152–68.

Friedman, Lester, David Desser, Sarah Kozloff, Martha Nochimson, and Stephen Prince. *An Introduction to Film Genre*. New York: Norton, 2013.

Gaines, Cork. "The Average College Football Team Makes More Money than the Next 20 College Sports Combined." *Business Insider* 20 Oct. 2016.

Glanville, Doug. "Who Gets to Call the Game?" *New York Times* 29 July 2017.

Golliver, Ben. "Bryant Gumbel Evokes Slavery in Rant against David Stern." *CBSSports.com / Cleveland 19 News* 19 Oct. 2011. Web.

Grindon, Leger. *Knockout: The Boxer and Boxing in American Cinema*. Jackson: U of Mississippi P, 2011.

Gurney, Gerald, Donna A. Lopiano, and Andrew Zimbalist. *Unwinding Madness: What Went Wrong with College Sports and How to Fix It*. Washington, DC: Brookings Institution Press, 2017.

Guttmann, Allen. *The Erotic in Sports*. New York: Columbia UP, 1996.

Hampton, Liz. "Women Comprise Nearly Half of NFL Audience, More Wanted." *Reuters* 4 Feb. 2017.

Harriot, Michael. "Just a Reminder: The NCAA Is a Plantation, and the Players Are Its Sharecroppers." *The Root* 31 Mar. 2017. Web.

Heywood, Leslie, and Shari L. Dworkin. *Built to Win: The Female Athlete as Cultural Icon*. Minneapolis: U of Minnesota P, 2003.

Hogan, Lawrence D., and Jules Tygiel. *Shades of Glory: The Negro Leagues and the Story of African-American Baseball*. Washington, DC: National Geographic Books, 2007.

Huizinga, Johan. *Homo Ludens: A Study of the Play-Element in Culture*. London: Routledge and Kegan Paul, 1938.

Jacoby, Susan. *Why Baseball Matters*. New Haven, CT: Yale UP, 2018.

Kang, Jay Caspian. "Could Legalized Gambling Save Us from the Insufferability of Fantasy Sports?" *New York Times* 30 Apr. 2017.

Landers, Chris. "Kevin Costner Wants to Make One Last Baseball Movie, Probably about the Cubs." *Cut4* 15 Apr. 2016.

Lauletta, Tyler "These Are the 20 Highest-Paid Athletes in the World." *Business Insider* 8 June 2017.

Leonard, David J. "'Is This Heaven?': White Sporting Masculinities and the Hollywood Imagination." *Visual Economies of/in Motion: Sport and Film*. Ed. C. Richard King and David J. Leonard. New York: Peter Lang, 2006. 165–94.

Leonard, David J. *Playing While White: Privilege and Power on and off the Field*. Seattle: U of Washington P, 2017.

Malamud. Bernard. *The Natural*. New York: Harcourt, Brace, 1952.

Mandell, Arnold J. "A Psychiatric Study of Professional Football." *Saturday Review/World* 5 Oct. 1974.

Maraniss, David. *Barack Obama: The Story*. New York: Simon and Schuster, 2013.

Marzorati, Gerald. *Late to the Ball: Age. Learn. Fight. Love. Play Tennis*. New York: Scribner, 2016.

McDaniel, Douglas. "Jacques Barzin, 'Baseball's Best Cultural Critic,' Turns His Back on the Game." *Bleacher Report* 6 July 2009. Web.

McDaniels, Pellom, III. "Filling in the Gaps and Recovering the Narratives of America's Forgotten Heroes." *All-Stars and Movie Stars: Sports in Film and History*. Ed. Ron Briley, Michael K. Schoenecke, and Deborah A. Carmichael. Lexington: U of Kentucky P, 2008. 129–54.

Messner, Michael A. *Out of Play: Critical Essays on Gender and Sport*. Albany: SUNY P, 2007.

———. *Power at Play: Sports and the Problem of Masculinity*. Boston: Beacon, 1992.

Miller, Andrew. "Winning It All: The Cinematic Construction of the Athletic American Dream." *American Dreams: Dialogues in U.S. Studies*. Ed. Ricardo Miguez. Newcastle, UK: Cambridge Scholars, 2007. 103–21.

Nadel, Alan. *Flatlining on the Field of Dreams: Cultural Narratives in the Films of President Reagan's America*. New Brunswick, NJ: Rutgers UP, 1998.

Oates, Joyce Carol. *On Boxing*. Garden City, NY: Dolphin/ Doubleday, 1987.

Obama, Barack. *Dreams from My Father*. New York: Times Books, 1995.

Orbach, Barak Y. "The Johnson-Jeffries Fight 100 Years Thence: The Johnson-Jeffries Fight and the Censorship of Black Superiority." *New York University Journal of Law & Liberty* 5.270 (2012): 270–346.

Orwell, George. "The Sporting Spirit." *Tribune* 14 Dec. 1945.

Peterson, Robert. *Only the Ball Was White: A History of Legendary Black Players and All-Black Professional Teams*. New York: Oxford University Press, 1992.

Pomerance., Murray "The Dramaturgy of Action and Involvement in Sports Film." *Quarterly Review of Film and Video* 23.4 (2006): 311–29.

Quote Garden. "Quotations about Football (American) and a Few on Rugby, Too." Web.

Roark, David. "The Decline of Baseball—and American Character." *The Week* 11 May 2015.

Roth, Philip. "My Baseball Years." *New York Times* 2 Apr. 1973.

Russo, Richard. *The Destiny Thief: Essays on Writing, Writers and Life*. New York: Knopf, 2018.

Sandomir, Richard. *The Pride of the Yankees: Lou Gehrig, Gary Cooper, and the Making of a Classic*. New York: Hachette Books, 2017.

Scanlon, Thomas. *Eros and Greek Athletics*. New York: Oxford UP, 2002.

Schwartz, Nick. "How Much Does a 2019 Super Bowl Commercial Cost." *For the Win* 3 Feb. 2019.

Sobchack, Vivian. "Baseball in the Post-American Cinema, or Life in the Minor Leagues." *East-West Film Journal* 7.1 (1993): 1–23.

Sperber, Murray. *Beer and Circus: How Big-Time Sports Is Crippling Undergraduate Education*. New York: Holt, 2001.

Spielberg, Steven. Interview. *Vega* 1993.

Streible, Dan. "A History of the Boxing Film, 1894–1915: Social Control and Social Reform in the Progressive Era." *Film History* 3 (1989): 235–57.

Thorn, John. "Baseball Film to 1920." *Our Game* 22 May 2012. Web.

Tomasulo, Frank P. "1976: Movies and Cultural Contradictions." *America Cinema of the 1970: Themes and Variations*. Ed. Lester D. Friedman. New Brunswick, NJ: Rutgers UP, 2007. 157–81.

Tudor, Deborah. "Hoosiers: The Race, Religion, and Ideology of Sports." *Jump Cut* 3 (Feb. 1988): 2–9.

Unterberger, Andrew. "How 90s Basketball Movies Explain 90s Basketball Culture." *theScore* 18 July 2014.

Wolff, Alexander. *The Audacity of Hoop: Basketball and the Age of Obama*. Philadelphia: Temple UP, 2015.

Zucker, Harvey Marc, and Lawrence J. Babich. *Sports Films: A Complete Reference*. Jefferson, NC: McFarland, 1987.

SELECTED FILMOGRAPHY

Any Given Sunday (Oliver Stone, 1999)

Bang the Drum Slowly (John D. Hancock, 1973)

Bend It like Beckham (Gurinder Chadha, 2002)

The Bingo Long Traveling All-Stars & Motor Kings
    (John Badham, 1976)

Blue Chips (William Friedkin, 1994)

Body and Soul (Robert Rossen, 1947)

Bull Durham (Ron Shelton, 1988)

Chariots of Fire (Hugh Hudson, 1981)

Coach Carter (Thomas Carter, 2005)

Eight Men Out (John Sayles, 1988)

Everybody's All-American (Taylor Hackford, 1988)

The Express (Gary Fleder, 2008)

Fat City (John Huston,1972)

Field of Dreams (Phil Alden Robinson, 1989)

Fight Club (David Fincher, 1999)

Friday Night Lights (Peter Berg, 2004)

Girlfight (Karyn Kusama, 2000)

Glory Road (James Gartner, 2006)

Golden Boy (Rouben Mamoulian, 1939)

He's Got Game (Spike Lee, 1998)

Hoop Dreams (Steve James, 1994)

Hoosiers (David Anspaugh, 1986)

The Jackie Robinson Story (Alfred E. Green, 1950)
Jim Thorpe: All American (Michael Curtiz, 1951)
Knute Rockne All American (Lloyd Bacon, 1940)
A League of Their Own (Penny Marshall, 1992)
The Longest Yard (Robert Aldrich, 1974)
Million Dollar Baby (Clint Eastwood, 2004)
Mystery, Alaska (Jay Roach, 1999)
The Natural (Barry Levinson, 1984)
North Dallas Forty (Ted Kotcheff, 1979)
Pat and Mike (George Cukor, 1952)
Personal Best (Robert Towne, 1982)
Pride of the Yankees (Sam Wood, 1942)
Raging Bull (Martin Scorsese, 1980)
Remember the Titans (Boaz Yakin, 2000)
Rocky (John G. Avildsen, 1976)
Rudy (David Anspaugh, 1993)
The Sandlot (David Mickey Evans, 1993)
Tin Cup (Ron Shelton, 1996)
Varsity Blues (Brian Robbins, 1999)
When We Were Kings (Leon Gast, 1996)
White Men Can't Jump (Ron Shelton, 1992)
The Wrestler (Darren Aronofsky, 2008)

INDEX

ABOUT THE AUTHOR

Lester D. Friedman is an emeritus professor and former chair of the Media and Society Program at Hobart and William Smith Colleges. Prior to his time at HWS, he taught cinema studies at Syracuse, Northwestern, and American Universities, as well as the Art Institute of Chicago. The author, coauthor, or editor of over twenty books, his work includes volumes on film genres, American cinema of the 1970s, American Jewish cinema, British film of the 1980s, Steven Spielberg, Peter Pan, Frankenstein, and Clint Eastwood. He has authored two produced screenplays and is a *Jeopardy!* champion.